# CLICKS, TRICKS, & GOLDEN HANDCUFFS
## 5-Point Roadmap for Tech Executives to Land Big-Impact Roles

MONIQUE MONTANINO

Resumé Tech Guru Publishing ■ Seattle, Washington

RESUMÉ TECH
G U R U

**Clicks, Tricks, & Golden Handcuffs**

As a certified career coach, I provide advice that may help you in your technology executive job search. This book does not guarantee that you will secure a role. Since I am not an attorney, I cannot provide you with legal advice, but I can suggest hiring one for executive employment contracts.

I changed all my clients' names and titles to protect their privacy. Client conversations in the book are based upon my notes and discussion recollections since there is no audio or video recording trail. The information in this book was correct at the time of publication and I am not at liberty to assume any liability for loss or damage caused by errors or omissions.

Here is a shout out to the geographically dispersed creative phenoms who collaborated on my brain dropping dream.

- Cover art design by Stephanie Corbin (Texas)
- Editing and book layout by Emily Fuggetta (Oregon)
- Photo image © by Sasha Reiko Photography (Washington)

Publisher's Cataloging-in-Publication Data

- Name: Montanino, Monique, author.
- Title: ***Clicks, Tricks, & Golden Handcuffs***: 5-Point Roadmap for Tech Executives to Land Big-Impact Roles / Monique Montanino.
- Description: Seattle, WA: Resumé Tech Guru Publishing, 2021 | Includes bibliography.
- Library of Congress Control Number: 2021921794
- Hardback: ISBN 978-1-7377462-4-9

- Paperback: ISBN 978-1-7377462-0-1 | ISBN 978-1-7377462-1-8
- Ebook: ISBN 978-1-7377462-2-5| ISBN 978-1-7377462-3-2

BISAC Categories

- BUS012020 | BUSINESS & ECONOMICS / Careers / Interviewing
- BUS037020 | BUSINESS & ECONOMICS / Careers / Job Hunting
- BUS056030 | BUSINESS & ECONOMICS / Careers / Resumes
- BUS071000 | BUSINESS & ECONOMICS / Leadership
- BUS106000 | BUSINESS & ECONOMICS / Mentoring & Coaching
- BUS107000 | BUSINESS & ECONOMICS / Personal Success

*For Pat. My favorite husband, personal chef, and fellow global explorer.*

# Table of Contents

# INTRODUCTION

If you are at a crossroads in your technology career and struggle with how to prepare for the next role, you arrived at the right place. Whether you are trapped at a company after a decade of service, passed over for executive positions, or your role is being eliminated, this book provides guidance to navigate forward.

My passion is supporting clients in pursuing their career dreams; it allows me to collaborate with innovative intellectuals who share intriguing stories about accomplishments in technology, team empowerment, and societal impact.

While innovators at business positioning for products and ideas, my clients are challenged with how to do that for themselves. Does that sound like you too?

***Clicks, Tricks, & Golden Handcuffs*** is an anthology of over 80 LinkedIn articles and blogs I wrote for technology executives to aid in their job search strategy. Over the past three years, these writings accrued over 20,000 views and, in part, drew over 200 clients to my consulting practice.

With my office door propped open, you can listen in on the highlight reel from executive conversations with CEOs, General Managers, Vice Presidents, and Directors pursuing opportunities outside of Amazon, IBM, Intel, Microsoft, and Seattle startups. You will gain insight on how to become an online click magnet for executive recruiters and the tricks for a successful job search strategy.

After all, are you not interested in securing your pair of golden handcuffs—an executive compensation package with equity—at a technology company?

If you are a current or aspiring executive seeking to land your role as a technology provocateur—a big-impact maker—at a Fortune 500, multinational company, or startup, this book offers ideas for:

- defining your career vision,
- positioning your brand for career opportunities,
- optimizing your resume and LinkedIn profile,
- honing your interviewing skills, and, most importantly,
- executing your plan for success.

It all started innocently enough. A decade later, at a tech Fortune 500 company, I was ensconced in golden handcuffs. For those of you unfamiliar with the term "golden handcuffs," it refers to the financial seduction corporations use to retain their highly compensated employees, so they do not leave for the competition.

I wore my golden handcuffs for 18 years, lured by cash bonuses, stock options, a pension, and the promise of retiree healthcare insurance. It allowed me to retire early and pursue a new avenue as a certified executive career coach three years ago.

My golden handcuffs slipped on when I was offered an executive relocation package from a Fortune 500 company. I moved from Dallas to Kansas City to work at Sprint's corporate headquarters with a compensation offer featuring paid expenses to offset a new home purchase and sell my existing one.

Five years with Sprint in the Midwest zipped by before I migrated like a salmon to Seattle. My career peaked in 2016 as a CenturyLink technology sales executive when I landed in the top 3% corporate-wide for annual sales quota attainment. After 18 years in technology, I slipped off my golden hand-cuffs and retired early at 55 years old.

Now what? Finally, I was going to commence on my top 10 global travel bucket list. In preparation, I took an 8-week in-person Italian language course before living for a month in Palermo, Sicily. It was invigorating, soaking up ancient culture and new experiences before returning to the U.S.

My life back home entailed volunteering as a career advocate in downtown Seattle at Uplift Northwest, a century-old non-profit that started during the Great Depression. For those experiencing homelessness, Uplift Northwest provides clients a temporary staffing agency and a supportive employment program along with hot meals and basic medical care. After moving on to do the same volunteering as a career advocate at non-profit Dress for Success, which supports female economic empowerment, I was restless.

Does it infuriate you when your mother is right? Mine told me I would be bored in retirement, and her proclamation only took a year and a half to be confirmed. Armed with my pro bono career-consulting knowledge, I made a career pivot, becoming a certified career coach for tech executives. Since I am primarily based in Seattle, my clients are the usual suspects employed in the Northwest. Over the past three years, my client base expanded across the U.S. from the West Coast to the East Coast and internationally.

The contents of this book correspond to a 5-point roadmap for obtaining your next tech executive role. You will begin with identifying your career vision and culminate with an implementation plan to execute that vision. It is the same method used in collaborating with my executive clients.

1. **Career Path**: develop your career vision, confront indecision, evaluate corporate versus startup roles, and consider remote positions
2. **C-Suite Advice**: think like a CEO, benefit from mentor and coach collaborations,

invest in your continuing education, and
join boards for networking opportunities
and social impact
3. **Personal Brand**: harness your superpower,
identify your top skills, create an elevator
pitch, embrace social media, and address
diversity and inclusion
4. **Job Search Tools**: investigate the best
practices for executive resumes, LinkedIn
profiles, interviews, and executive
compensation
5. **Strategy Implementation**: create a
project plan, take a potential sabbatical,
focus on job search execution, and make
yourself a priority!

## Exclusive Workbook Companion: Before You Start Reading Further

Before creating your career vision statement,
request the workbook companion, exclusively available to you as a purchaser of *Clicks, Tricks, &
Golden Handcuffs*. It is a consolidation of all the
end-of-chapter exercises that appear in this book.
Please access *www.resumetech.guru* and send a workbook request via the contact tab located on the
menu. For the subject line, type "*Golden Handcuffs
Workbook.*"

You will begin writing out your career vision and end
with your successful implementation plan. Each
section contains four chapters. After reading each
chapter, please complete the exercise that appears at
the end.

We are off on your career journey adventure; it's time to reflect on your **Career Path**!

# Career Roadmap Point #1
# Career Path

While my clients earn six- or even seven-figure salaries at top tech companies, when they contact me, they are looking for their next roles. Money aside, what you may have in common with them is a desire to fine-tune your job search strategy.

Whether you are at the early stages of your career, mid-point, or heading into retirement, it is reasonable to be at an impasse. I will share industry best practices, academic research, executive client stories, my career path journey, and interactive exercises to support your efforts. After all, knowledge is power.

Do you have colleagues and friends that you admire who have career magic? You know, the ones who are destined to run corporations or consultancies? They seem to have it figured out.

That was not the case for me since I have zigged and zagged over the past 30 years like a skier traversing a snow-covered mountain. My career crisscrossed from consumer brand consulting, B2B (business-to-business) telecom marketing, and enterprise technology sales to executive career coaching. This route is derived from a combination of education, training, planning, serendipity, mentorship, perseverance, and risk-taking marked with laughter and, frankly, some crying along the way when it came to the sales quota.

At this first roadmap point for your **Career Path**, I will discuss how to:

- develop your career vision,
- confront indecision,
- evaluate corporate versus startups roles, and
- consider executive remote positions.

At the end of the chapter there is an exercise to apply your knowledge. Once again, you can request your exclusive companion workbook at *www. resumetech.guru*.

# CAREER VISION

When I was a teenager, I envisioned myself as a journalist or attorney, not a technology sales executive. Unlike some of my clients raised overseas, my European parents were not guiding me on career choices. There was no mistake that my parents wanted me to go to college and were generously funding that mission, but they felt it was my responsibility to determine the course of action. I had my eyes focused on attending Harvard, Rice, or The University of Texas at Austin.

Looking back, my early childhood career role models might have been what I watched on TV sitting in our living room in Houston, Texas. It was before Netflix was invented and streaming services took off. Showing my age here, perhaps Perry Mason and Walter Cronkite filled my unconscious? Men with integrity and influence because, shocker, women typically were not working outside the home in the '70s; how times have changed! The irony is that I did not become a journalist or an attorney. However, I write for a living like a journalist. Plus, I create and read contracts, as would an attorney.

So, the question is, how did I get here? I turned to an expert.

Psychologist Mark Savickas is chair emeritus and professor at the Northeastern Ohio Universities College of Medicine. As a research-based career development expert, he developed the *"Theory of Work Adjustment."* It provides a rational framework for implementing a career choice. He and I share a dislike of the Myers-Briggs approach for summing you up with a mere four letters. If you are a fan of personality types or want to learn more, you will dive deeper into the Myers-Briggs categories in the next chapter. Plus, there is a free personality assessment quiz.

Getting back to Dr. Savickas, he believes:

> "An individual's career pattern—that is, the occupational level attained and the sequence, frequency, and duration of jobs—is determined by the parent's socioeconomic level and the person's education, abilities, personality traits, self-concepts, and career adaptability ... with the opportunities presented."[1]

If you are like me, you probably did not think about how you arrived at your current role in tech. Working with me, it is one of the first questions you will be asked. Sometimes, it makes for an excellent backdrop for your personal brand. For example, one client born in Australia was an avid wooden boat builder. Oliver (not his real name to protect client confidentiality) turned that building passion into three different serial startup adventures before coming ashore to the U.S. After his proverbial ship sailed at Amazon, we joined forces for his next move navigating the waters to early-phase startup companies. In turn, his LinkedIn profile and interviewing bio focus on his builder persona. We will revisit Oliver's final answer on choosing between a FinTech and augmented reality startup within the executive compensation chapter.

The other question I always ask in my initial 30-minute career consult is, "So, what do you want to be when you grow up?"

It scratches the surface of a client's career vision. Inevitably, after 5 to 15 years at a particular company, your passion wanes related to:

- your perceived diluted impact,
- an uninspiring company culture,
- a work balance that has gone haywire, or
- being passed over for the next promotion.

My client Raj lost his passion as an executive in Seattle, burnt out by his business unit's toxic culture and a lack of a promotion path. Instead of a lengthy career at a single company, Raj had worked at 12 different companies in 24 years, including startups, consulting companies, and two Fortune 500 companies. Raj attained a solid academic foundation with an MS in Computer Science. His LinkedIn profile featured many endorsements for software development and engineering skills. Plus, he had highly regarded certifications for Certified Information Security Professional (CISSP) and Project Management Professional (PMP).

I asked Raj my go-to "What do you want to be when you grow up?" question in our initial phone conversation.

Without hesitation, he responded, "I want to be an agent of change. My checklist includes obtaining a VP slot and managing a P&L (profit and loss) at a smaller-size company."

He had specific thoughts about companies and culture for his next role but struggled to create his online persona and tell his story on paper. Sound familiar?

During our coaching sessions, Raj and I further fleshed out his career vision through a questionnaire review. You might wonder where he is now, and that answer is revealed momentarily.

In this chapter, you will gain **Career Vision** insight on how to:

- build a framework for your executive career,
- clarify your non-negotiables for company selection, and
- create a succinct career vision statement for job guidance.

Your career vision is related to developing your personal brand by creating a mental image of the future. It describes the absolute peak of where you envision yourself in your career. To plan, it stands to reason you need a destination. Consider your vision to be the North Star for mapping out your career success strategy.

## UNCOVERING MY FRAMEWORK

As a corporate brand consultant for Coca-Cola, General Motors, and the U.S. Army, I was at a road-block in my career. After achieving co-owner status as the president of The Dallas Research Centre, the work became robotic, and I was exhausted by extensive global sojourns, so I checked out of my company at 29 years old. I took a 6-month sabbatical to ponder my next move. It led to a marketing research consulting contractor role, which blossomed within three months into a full-time employee position at Nortel Networks. After seven years of employment, I walked away with stock options and my first pension from the now-defunct Canada-based multinational corporation.

My next career foray landed me at two Fortune 500 telecommunication companies, Sprint and Century-Link. For 18 years, I went on autopilot since new positions landed organically, with no proper planning.

"I was just tapped on the shoulder for the next role" is a common refrain I hear from clients with 10-25 years of service at one company.

After fully vesting in the Sprint 401K, while spending five years in Kansas City, I had an incredible opportunity to continue working for Sprint while living on the Olympic Peninsula in Washington State. My new remote work location was in Port Ludlow, located two hours northwest of Seattle near Canada, entailing a car ride and a ferry to reach the final destination on the aptly named Paradise Bay Road.

As part of our retirement vision, my husband and I built our dream home in a rural county with a small population of 27,000. It was so small that I was called for jury duty twice within two years, and one time my husband and I appeared on the same jury. I did not even think that was legal!

Within a couple of years, Sprint spun off its telephone landline business, and my new role emerged as the Northwest General Manager at the new entity named Embarq. Life was great since my purview covered Washington and Oregon, allowing me to explore our service areas, primarily in rural towns. In 2008 CenturyLink was created when CenturyTel acquired Embarq in an all-stock transaction for $6 billion.

My idyllic vision was abruptly interrupted when my boss called me and told me I had to move to CenturyLink's corporate headquarters in Monroe, Louisiana, to keep my job.

My non-negotiable was moving from my dream house, which lit my fire, so I hired a Seattle-based career coach and professional resume writer. I had two paths to explore—stay with the company or venture out to the competition. The coach's development process helped me fine-tune a career vision and a framework to move forward.

Ultimately, I stayed with CenturyLink, re-branded Lumen in 2020, in a new role as an enterprise sales executive for seven years. It made the best financial sense since I wrangled an early retirement at 55.

During a déjà vu moment last year, I went through this career vision process as part of my coaching certification and for a job interview. For the latter, deciding to be a contractor for a career outplacement company while still maintaining my practice, I developed two visions: personal and professional. It helped me determine the contractor job was not a healthy work-life balance opportunity, so I declined the offer.

## CORPORATE VISION AS CAREER INSPIRATION

Creating a career vision might sound challenging, so let's make it easy. For inspiration, check out what companies have developed. A corporate vision statement provides an aspirational description of what an organization would like to accomplish. It is the basis for choosing a course of action for executive leadership and employees.

Below is a broad selection of corporate visions to consider. My favorite is the first one—great sentiment plus cuts to the chase.

- **Life Is Good**: To spread the power of optimism.
- **Google**: To organize the world's information and make it universally accessible and useful.
- **Microsoft**: Our mission is to empower

every person and every organization on the planet to achieve more.
- **Walmart**: Be THE destination for customers to save money, no matter how they want to shop.

## RAJ'S CAREER VISION

In my practice, coaching begins with understanding a clear, compelling vision of what you want to achieve. On my first phone call with clients, we discuss their current job status, and then I ask them:

- What do you want to accomplish in your next role?
- What is standing in your way?
- Where are you on your journey?
- What is one thing you can do to move forward?
- What are your non-negotiables?
- What are your short to long-term goals?

After mutually determining we are compatible, my clients receive a 4-page custom questionnaire. Although Type A's think there is some magical equation for completion, it is merely a mechanism to guide our efforts.

The initial 1:1 video session with Raj began after he had filled out the questionnaire. The first question was designed to uncover his career vision, including his non-negotiables.

His dream was focused on innovative deliveries, moving quickly, and introducing novel technologies and implementations to market. He believed teams should be organized by product rather than discipline; in turn, the leadership of software development, hardware development, project management, Quality Assurance (QA), and customer service would converge under the same focal point. On the responsibility front, he wanted to own recruiting, retaining, and growing teams while representing the technical interests and image of the company at public events.

His ideal next step was to attain increased responsibilities in breadth and depth of technical ownership, ultimately culminating in a CTO role within five years.

After three weeks, I asked, "What did you gain from our time together?"

Raj replied, "That is easy. You organized my career transition next steps and decluttered a resume of 15 years with a laundry list of irrelevant skills. I now have a solidified career vision, strategy, and execution plan."

Now, it was his turn to drive his career vision map. With GPS turned on, five months later, Raj became a Director at Facebook.

## EXERCISE: PUT IT INTO PRACTICE

Before you create your career vision statement, access the workbook companion. It is available at *www.resumetech.guru*. Please send a workbook request via the contact tab and type *"Golden Handcuffs Workbook"* for the subject line.

Once you receive a copy, please go to the worksheet for **Roadmap #1: Career Vision** to complete the exercise below.

## Action Plan

Trying to resolve an issue or get success begins with a vision of what success looks like. Research shows you will be more likely to attain and apply a commitment to it if you have an easy-to-visualize goal. Let's walk through the framework to provide a clear and inspiring direction for your future.

To prime the pump, check out the following career vision examples. If you are in technology, do any of these resonate with you? Mine appears in the mix below; I bet you can spot it!

- I will become a well-known and respected cloud strategist in the tech industry.
- Be a CxO at a Fortune Global 2000 within the next year and retire at 60.
- Live as a global nomad, exploring new cultures on a 10-year travel bucket list while being a top career alchemist for technology executives.
- Be recognized as a leader in my organization, helping transform it into a culture respecting all its stakeholders—while being the best spouse and parent I can be.
- Be an honest, empathetic, and impactful machine learning expert and recognized internationally within my industry.
- Run an AI startup with a high product

metabolism that will significantly impact positive societal change.

The estimated completion time for this exercise is 45 minutes. Please take a couple of minutes per question to think and jot down your answers.

**Career Vision Framework Questions**

1. What makes me happy?
2. If I could swap places with a person, who would that be and why?
3. What is best for my family?
4. What are my values, including non-negotiables?
5. What inspires me?
6. How will I know I made it?
7. What is the legacy I want to leave behind?
8. What is my career aspiration?
9. What does financial security look like?

## YOUR CAREER VISION

By assembling your responses above, you can put it all together.

"I am a _____
who wants to be _____
_____."

By the way, career vision statements are fluid and change. I revisit mine and adjust when seeking guidance on decisions. It varies annually; yours might as well.

## KEY TAKEAWAYS

In this chapter for **Career Vision** insight, you learned about:

- building a framework for your executive career,
- clarifying your non-negotiables for company selection, and
- creating a succinct career vision statement for job guidance.

Now you have a career vision, but what happens when you can't decide whether to take the highway or side roads? For example, some clients think they need two different resumes for a VP of Engineering and a CIO role.

In the next chapter, we will walk through the importance of selecting a direction and giving it 100% before re-configuring your career GPS.

# INDECISION: CHOOSE A PATH

When making decisions about your subsequent career pursuit, do you vacillate between staying put at your current company and taking a leap into the unknown?

If it makes you feel any better, you are not alone. Hundreds of clients have reached out to me for what I call "fork-in-the-road" advice. Sometimes it's related to the type of company path to select, whether weighing options between a Fortune 500 company or a startup. Other times, it's keeping all their options open regarding the type and title of the role.

For example, Malcolm, a Senior Director of Go-to-Market Strategy who spent his entire 30-year career at Microsoft, teetered between companies and types of roles.

Probing into how to help during our initial call, Malcolm hesitated before stating, "I'm on the fence about whether to stay at Microsoft or move on to another company for my last hurrah."

To which I responded, "We certainly can work through the pros and cons of each. What type of role are you interested in?"

He said, "That is a tough question. I would consider Product Management or Integrated Partner Marketing roles. I believe I need 2 different resumes."

Although there is nothing wrong with multiple paths, my advice is to choose one before course-correcting. I explained to Malcolm that he might dilute his efforts without a proper focus and suggested we start with one resume. He concurred and selected a Partner Marketing approach.

You might be surprised at what happened next.

While we were finalizing the resume, his manager contacted him and told Malcolm his position was being eliminated. At this juncture, his options were to select the Microsoft severance package or take a chance to apply internally and find another job within the company.

Guess what? Now he is an executive in Partner Marketing at a competitor of Microsoft. This result came from actively networking outside of his corporate alma mater and finding a role addressing his career vision. Malcolm created a checklist of items to complete every day: reach out to colleagues regarding his pursuit of a new role, review potential job openings on career websites, apply for jobs online, and network with contacts at the hiring company. Armed with an offer from AWS and only a hope of securing a position at Microsoft, Malcolm selected the sure thing. Sometimes companies nudge you in a direction; after all, it is employment at will.

In this chapter related to **Indecision**, we will dive into the importance of how to:

- confront your career path indecision,
- select a career path with a strategic plan, and
- implement an action plan to move forward.

Never a wiz in biology, I do know the prefrontal cortex and hippocampus are the most critical parts of the human brain for decision making. Neuroscientist John-Dylan Haynes's experimental data reveals that your brain makes a decision a whole 10 seconds before you actually realize it.[1] This data challenges the notion that your decisions are totally conscious. While an interesting concept, the big conundrum is the components that lead up to your conclusion.

My clients are sometimes challenged in making decisions, big or small. Upon reflection, I noticed a common thread amongst them is a lack of something for decision making:

- confidence
- finances
- knowledge
- life experience
- mental health
- relationship support

- training

There is no magic decision wand. It is a personal journey, and sadly, some folks stay stuck in their careers. I understand hesitancy and have experienced most of the negatives stated above. Through it all, my motto is the most significant risks lead to immense rewards. It has served me well. What is your motto for decision-making? Do you have one?

## DECISION FATIGUE—EXPLAINED

Psychological evidence shows that decision quality declines after an extensive decision-making session, a phenomenon known as decision fatigue. Upon researching this topic, it appears to be a common occurrence. Has this happened to you?

In his book, "*Willpower: Rediscovering the Greatest Human Strength*," social psychologist Dr. Roy Baumeister discusses how our daily mental energy is finite.[2] The Freudian psychological description is ego depletion. Baumeister created a term for it called decision fatigue.

Decision fatigue does not appear to have age limits. CNBC contributor and San Francisco-based psychotherapist Tess Brigham cites research related to decision fatigue for her predominantly millennial patient base.[3] She says the major complaint she hears from patients is having too many choices and concern about making the wrong decision.

In 2017, RescueTime, a personal analytics service providing productivity software for workplace time management, analyzed over 225 million hours of their users' working time, finding their average user switches between tasks more than 300 times per day.[4] The result? Decision fatigue because of a lack of energy and focus.

The bottom line, too many decisions lead to not making any or making bad ones. For some people, there are alternatives. Read on for my fork-in-the-road experiences.

## DECISION-MAKING PROCESS

I can appreciate that not all people can readily vet a decision. Here is what has worked for me. It might help with your career choices.

- **Find Mentors**: I have always sought the advice and counsel of colleagues and executives I admire. It is refreshing to hear a different perspective. My husband happens to be my mentor as a former sales director and electrical engineer at both Fortune 500s and a San Jose startup. At times, I listened to the hard truth (which I did not enjoy hearing) to grow and prosper. I continue to do so today with other mentors as a continuous life learner.
- **Hire Experts**: To keep my job at CenturyLink, I was required to move from Seattle, Washington, to an isolated town down South. That is when I turned toward expert career guidance. I signed up for a job search site for marketing executives. Upon

using their resume assessment tool, it highlighted optimization areas that required a resume writer. My next step was hiring a career consultant and resume writer. After two weeks of assessment with a reformatted resume, I applied for jobs and saw immediate results. With my newfound confidence and enhanced online LinkedIn presence, job interviews materialized. Finally, I secured a new career adventure—ironically staying at my same company while transitioning from a marketing to a sales executive role. It worked out well for me—different from the planned path, but life is unpredictable.

- **Discuss with Family**: When I became a marketing consultant after graduate school, my mom advised me not to join the firm because of the principal owner's reputation. I vacillated about whether I should take the role but, in the end, overruled the maternal feedback. The consulting role became the best mentoring opportunity for me while working for a Ph.D. in statistics. Although my mentor was challenging, infuriating, and inappropriate at times during corporate meeting discussions, this experience catapulted me to become a consulting partner-owner at another firm five years later.

- **3 Decision Points**: I love three inputs on any decision because it provides different perspectives. In the past couple of years, I received three quotes each for the following projects—website development, hosting platforms, home repair, and a Prada purse purchase. I made decisions on all four items in less than a week. The Prada decision took the longest. I ponder discretionary fiscal decisions longer than business decisions. Do you share the same experience?

## PERSONALITY TYPES

My life has been an incredible roller coaster adventure in both my professional and personal life. I enjoy collaborating with unique individuals seeking a radical change from their current role, plus open to a city relocation. I fondly refer to them as "The Adventurers."

As mentioned in Chapter 1, I am not a fan of Myers-Briggs, although it provides a high-level classification of you within a team environment. Yet some of you have an affinity for Myers-Briggs and enjoy a test, so this section is dedicated to you.

If you worked at a Fortune 500 company, it is highly likely you took a Myers-Briggs personality assessment as part of a team building event. It is an item for leadership to check off for the annual performance review as being employee-focused. As team members, we shrugged since we were not sure how it helped with our professional collaboration or our upward mobility. I have never been great at remembering or caring about my alphabet soup of the following four criteria, which can change based upon the time of day or my mood:

- focus your attention or re-energize = extraversion (E) / introversion (I)
- perceive or take in information = sensing (S) / intuition (N)
- make decisions = thinking (T) / feeling (F)
- orient yourself to the outside world = judgment (J) / perception (P)

To frame it up, only 9% of the population is The Adventurer = ISFP. According to the 16 Personalities website, an ISFP characterizes someone who redefines conventional beauty and behavior.[5] They refuse to be boxed in by limitations, and they love to experiment with who they are, what they can do, and what is expected of them. For me, they are fantastic individuals to hang out with for a positive perspective on life. Their unconventional approach may limit an early retirement goal, but we don't all want that path.

If you do not have access to Myers-Briggs, you can head over for a free analysis at *www.16personalities.com* for an approximate 12-minute test. It is fun, easy, and provides you with a high-level assessment. Since I do not ponder these questions for long, you might have the same experience as I did, only taking five minutes for your results. According to this personality test, an Adventurer Profile (ISFP-A / ISFP-T) has the following traits:

- **Strengths**: Charming, sensitive to others, imaginative, passionate, curious, artistic
- **Weaknesses**: Fiercely independent,

unpredictable, easily stressed, overly competitive, fluctuating self-esteem

Most of my executive clients have established lives grounded by family concerns to stay put, but some take a leap of faith. Depending on your age or health, you have a finite time enjoying your next 10-30 professional years. If you can, why not do the extraordinary and go on an adventure?

## EXERCISE: PUT IT INTO PRACTICE

You will continue to evolve professionally and personally. Careers are not linear, and neither are you. Enjoy what you do professionally 40-60 hours weekly. And, yes, some of you put in far more time than that.

Seek out your new adventure, whether that is within your current company or on an alternative path. Sometimes the title or the salary is not what it is cracked up to be, but life is for enjoyment with friends and family, not just work.

Please go to your worksheet for **Roadmap #1: Indecision** to complete the exercise below.

**Action Plan**

1. Your Career Vision: Copy what you created in the first chapter for your career vision.

2. Mission statement: Describe what you do, for whom, and how.

3. Core values: List the top 5 beliefs and behaviors to achieve your vision and mission.

    a) Behavior & traits; e.g., integrity, perseverance, positivity
    b) Rights & causes; e.g., altruism, community development, stewardship
    c) Life; e.g., family, honesty, healthy work-life balance

4. Strength

    a) How would your boss or employee describe you?
    b) What skills have you worked to develop?
    c) What are your talents or natural-born gifts?

5. Weakness

    a) What are your negative work habits?
    b) Is there a gap in your education or training?
    c) How would others describe your weakness?

6. Opportunity

    a) What is a growth industry for your subsequent employment?
    b) Is there new technology in your industry?
    c) Are you able to move to another state or out of the country for employment?

7. Threat

a) Is your industry changing direction?
b) Is there intense competition for jobs you
are best suited to?
c) What is the most significant external
danger to your goals?

8. For your short-term goals, what career lane do you
want to select?

a) Develop 2 actionable tactics you can do
this month; e.g., reach out to a contact at a
company for employment opportunities,
resume revamp, find a mentor.
b) Put a timeline on each item.
c) Then execute one tactic this week. If you
fail, try something new. What do you have to
lose?

9. For your long-term goals, what do you want to
achieve in 10-15 years?

a) Create a list of items you need to complete
in the long term; e.g., education, certification, move to another city, retirement.
b) Put a timeline on each item.

## KEY TAKEAWAYS

In this chapter related to **Indecision**, you learned
about:

- confronting your career path indecision,
- selecting a career path with a strategic
  plan, and

- implementing an action plan to move forward.

I picked paths against advice and went for it. The bottom line, there were significant finances and personal commitments that did not work out perfectly, but the upside was worthwhile. Life is messy not black and white.

Choose a path.

Would you like to listen in on a private conversation with a Microsoft General Manager who leaped to a startup? Then it is time to begin the next chapter.

# CORPORATE VERSUS STARTUP

In your next career adventure, you may think about the job opportunity, title, promotion, benefits, and culture. These days importance is given to a laundry list of items from remote working, stock options, or equity positions to bringing your new pandemic puppy to the workplace.

During my initial consultation with clients, we discuss what pathway they are considering. Since my practice focuses on technology executives, four major tracks appear: 1) transitioning from one Fortune 500 to another, 2) moving from a Fortune 500 to a startup, 3) traversing the other direction from startup to Fortune 500, and 4) moving into a consulting role.

My clients have definite views about their comfort level being employed by a Fortune 500 versus a startup related to their age, family considerations, and financial risk tolerance.

As promised in the previous chapter, it is time to listen in on a private conversation with Kapil, the Microsoft General Manager leaping to a Series G startup. We initially met at the start of 2020; four months later, he followed up with me. He hired another resume writer within that time, but Kapil was not gaining any traction with his new document.

Kapil sheepishly asked, "I know I probably should have gone with you to begin with for my personal branding. Would you mind reviewing my two resumes and letting me know what is not working?"

Looking back to the choose a path discussion from our last chapter, my observations for Kapil:

> "Your LinkedIn profile does not match the two versions of your resume since a VP of Product Management is quite different from a VP of Strategic Planning & Execution. Recruiters are confused about your direction."

He agreed, saying, "One of my colleagues told me my social media profile needs to be updated. What should I do?"

I countered, "Let's start with your career vision and focus on moving to a startup. From there, we can update your resume along with your online profile."

Kapil surprised me with his timeline, casually mentioning, "I need the resume update in five days since I'm interviewing with a startup."

My internal thought: "You want it when?"

Although Kapil secured a startup interview, the timeline was troublesome for me since I was completely booked for the week. The best I could offer was a final resume within 10 days. After a couple of revisions, we landed on an umbrella positioning for Kapil as a Chief Product Officer with expertise in strategy, product marketing, and product management.

Upon asking Kapil if he needed to practice his interviewing techniques, he shared his confidence in interviewing at this Series G startup related to an acquaintance with the founders. A previous boss had reached out to Kapil regarding the opportunity, and this recruiting activity was being conducted in stealth mode. He was adamant that he was guaranteed to get this opportunity.

In April 2021, the startup Kapil discussed went IPO, valued at $8 billion, and is now listed on the NYSE. Whether based on the compensation package or his interviewing skills, Kapil is not part of the executive team; he is still at Microsoft. It is unclear to me exactly what occurred since Kapil has not reached out to me post interview. The irony is that his LinkedIn profile did not change, based upon a 4-page guideline I developed for him. It proves the adage that "you can lead a horse to water, but you cannot make it drink."

In this chapter, I will touch upon **Corporate versus Startup** opportunities to:

- address the pros and cons of the two types of companies,

- share startup resources, and
- identify your top three companies.

## TAKING THE CORPORATE PATH

If you are tired of the volatility of startups, here are six considerations for joining an established corporation, whether privately held or traded on Wall Street.

**Pros**

- **Financial Stability**: A majority of my clients have near-term college-bound children. Hence, a Fortune 500 company or mid-size corporation with a decade of profitability growth provides them financial peace of mind. Typically, working for a Fortune 500 leads to a longer-term commitment based upon vesting periods for stock options, equity, 401Ks, and pensions. I will go into more detail about who is still offering pensions later in this chapter.
- **Executive-Level Roles**: I am amazed when my clients speak numerically regarding job roles at a competitor. For example, Microsoft Senior Director to Executive VP positions generally fall between the 67-81 levels. As employees rise in the ranks, more of their total compensation comes in stock, while cash bonuses remain stable. Compared to a startup with an executive title attached to a broader scope of responsibilities, I have

noticed a Fortune 500 role has a tighter range of duties for a specific product, program, or domain.

- **Resources**: One of my serial startup clients mentioned he missed the luxury of having Microsoft office supplies in addition to training programs, people resources, and financial capital. It was a light bulb moment since my experience was similar at Sprint and CenturyLink for ordering office supplies online or asking an administrative assistant for support. When it came to employee resources or budget, I created a business case to obtain required resources. I realized that in the fourth quarter of the business calendar, expense budgets always tightened up or vanished, but imagine that experience every day at a startup? Nerve-racking.

## Cons

- **Layoffs**: Jobs are routinely moved or eliminated at a Fortune 500 company. Every year while at Sprint or CenturyLink, there were employee layoffs. My least favorite activity was stack ranking employees and then informing individuals about their role elimination, especially around the holidays. The executive level is not exempt from layoffs, primarily when M&A (merger & acquisition) occurs. I experienced the tumultuous impact of six events across 18 years when a spin-off or merger occurred.

There were always redundancies since, after all, that is one of the ways to reduce operating expenses to report improved results on Wall Street. This is also called "managing to the stock price."

- **Office Politics**: Over the years, I learned the value of executive sponsorship, making or breaking your career growth. I hear from clients that their sponsor left or was let go; the client no longer had a career cheerleader in the house. Startups are bare-bones, with the VCs (venture capitalists) and the executives to contend with, so you know where you stand in the equation.

- **Less Nimble in Implementations**: Incubators and think tanks exist within Fortune 500 environments, but that does not mean customer solutions go to market quickly. The business case approval process for product enhancements or new solution offerings does not occur within one month, while startups can turn on the dime with fewer executive inputs because there is less red tape in a lean organization.

## WHO IS STILL OFFERING PENSIONS?

A pension provides monthly retirement income, but not all employers offer pensions. Government organizations and some large companies offer a pension. Employee benefits firm Willis Towers Watson noted that within the past 17 years, companies providing traditional pension plans to new hires fell from 50% to 5%.[1] The great news is there are still companies offering them. Think about a 5-year career investment yielding a retirement benefit to you in your 50s. To pay for retirement healthcare insurance, I exercised my CenturyLink pension at 55. I'm waiting another decade before I do the same with my Nortel Networks pension.

My Nortel pension did not go away because, even if a company goes bankrupt and out of business, the U.S. government handles pension insurance through the Pension Benefit Guaranty Corporation (PBGC), although there is a cap on payout amount.

According to the PBGC website, they "protect the retirement security of nearly 37 million Americans in single employer and multiemployer pension plans."[2]

I am quite thankful.

If you are a tech person, I strongly urge you to check out the following companies offering pensions since it will help you in retirement, even if it is not as intriguing as working for AWS, Google, Facebook, or Microsoft. Future ROI (return on investment) is as essential as resume building with hot tech companies. You can still join those later. The following U.S.-based companies offer fully funded pensions for new hires with a tenure ranging from 2 to 5 years noted below if publicly disclosed.

- Aflac (Columbus, GA)
- BB&T (Winston-Salem, NC): 5 years
- Coca-Cola (Atlanta, GA): 2 years
- Eli Lilly & Co. (Indianapolis, IN)
- ExxonMobil (Irving, TX): 5 years
- JM Family Enterprise (Deerfield Beach, FL)
- Johnson & Johnson (New Brunswick, NJ): 5 years
- JPMorgan Chase (NYC, NY): 3 years
- Merck (Kenilworth, NJ): 5 years
- NextEra Energy (Juno Beach, FL): 3 years
- NuStar Energy (San Antonio, TX)
- PG&E (San Francisco, CA): 5 years
- Prudential (Newark, NJ)

## CONSIDERATIONS FOR JOINING STARTUPS

If you knew there was a 10% success rate for the company you were interested in working for, what decision-making criteria would you use?

According to Failory, a content site for startup founders and entrepreneurs, 90% of global startups fail.[3] Of course, there is more to that statistic regarding the industry, geographic location, and customer offerings. There are distinct camps of people choosing to work within or outside a startup.

The startup path requires several considerations for my tech executive clients. If you are pondering the startup route, here are six pros and cons I have uncovered.

**Pros**

- **Making an Impact**: Do you sometimes feel as though you are trying to boil the ocean versus making a great cup of coffee when it comes to your job? In a startup environment, typically, you have a significant opportunity to impact strategic direction, vision, and mission if you are on the ground floor of the company's inception.

- **Adrenaline Rush**: Do you recall the first time you started something new and experienced those butterflies of excitement? Here is an outlet for recreating that experience with charting an unknown course with the next new service or product that fulfills a customer need.

- **Upside Potential**: Unlike companies who have structured criteria for compensation and promotions, there is an opportunity, if things are going well, for a quicker ascent to the top to move into a CxO position with additional equity payout and responsibility. I have yet to meet a client that wanted to downsize their title and role unless they were retiring.

## Cons

- **Smoke & Mirrors**: After 20 years at global companies, my husband was excited to accept an offer as a sales executive at an optical technology company. He fervently believed in the product potential. Several months into the role, he found an over-exuberance in every category from speed to market to manufacturing cost, cash flow requirements, and funding activities. It takes significant effort to build a company from ground zero, and you will not necessarily be aware of the positives or negatives before joining. So, make sure to ask critical questions regarding financials, targets, and milestones before accepting a role.

- **Executive Management**: In the past year, I have had several clients working at startups that imploded. Yes, they became unemployed. One recurring theme was that the original inventor had great ideas but was a less than stellar CEO. Why? In these situations, the owner had zero management leadership experience, and unfortunately, he did not hire an executive team to bring balance and optimize financial, operations, and sales functions.

- **Work-Life Unbalance**: In a smaller organization, there is a tendency to wear many hats, which might be your strength. On the flip side, starting new processes and building sales funnels can make for long hours into the nights and weekends. I have been at three startups and felt I was always thinking about optimization. For some, that might be exciting, or it may not be your cup of tea.

## STARTUP RESOURCES

If you are curious about what startups are available globally or locally in Seattle, there are many resources to begin your quest. If you are intrigued, my recommendation is to conduct your due diligence and reach out to a founder to have an informational discussion. Here are three websites I found that may aid in your search.

- **AngelList**: For tech and startup jobs
- **Built In Seattle**: Hub for Seattle startups and tech jobs
- **Startup Ranking**: Discover, rank, and prospect startups worldwide

## EXERCISE: PUT IT INTO PRACTICE

It is time to access your worksheet. Use **Roadmap #1: Corporate versus Startup** to complete the exercise below.

**Action Plan**

1. Create a list of your top 3 companies and explain why you are drawn to them.

    a)   Company #1 & why?
    b)   Company #2 & why?
    c)   Company #3 & why?

2. Find 3 job postings you are interested in.

    a)   Job URL #1

i. Top 3 skills you offer

ii. Write out a story that describes why you are the perfect fit; use this for your cover letter and interview response. Use the CAR approach: state the context of the situation, actions that you took, and the results you attained.

b)   Job URL #2

i. Top 3 skills you offer

ii. Write out a story that describes why you are the perfect fit; use this for your cover letter and interview response. Use the CAR approach.

c)   Job URL #3

i. Top 3 skills you offer

ii. Write out a story that describes why you are the perfect fit; use this for your cover letter and interview response. Use the CAR approach.

## KEY TAKEAWAYS

In this chapter for **Corporate versus Startup**, you learned about:

- addressing the pros and cons of the two types of companies,
- sharing startup resources, and
- identifying your top three companies.

If you completed the exercise, you now have: listed three companies to pursue, outlined the top skills you bring to the table, and developed a relevant leadership success story that you can leverage with a company during an interview.

In the next chapter, we will explore being a full-time executive in your favorite place on the earth. Where might that be?

**Bow down:**
Leigh Bowery,
Le Privilège,
Paris, 1988

## DON'T MISS IT...

There's still time to visit the exhibition celebrating the costumes of legendary performance artist Leigh Bowery at The Fitzrovia Chapel in Pearson Square. Bowery, who founded the Leicester Square nightclub Taboo in 1985, had a mantra for the sort of looks you were expected to pull to gain entry: 'Dress as though your life depends on it, or don't bother.' Bowery passed away in 1994 from Aids-related complications, but his work continues to inspire fashion designers working today, from Vivienne Westwood, Gareth Pugh and Kim Jones to Charles Jeffrey and Richard Quinn.

*Until 6 Feb (fitzroviachapel.org)*

rated bowling alley opened in
0. It consisted of 14 lanes, built
ld play in full circle skirts and
eam emblazoned on the back of
magine the Dior Vibe bag,
ri in a curvaceous bowling shape
f a vintage leather sneaker, firmly
. Tenpin Lanes closed in 1970 and
w stands on the site. Fortunately,
orial strike whether at Rowans,
n your local Sainsbury's.
g, £4,800, at Harrods (020 7730
rrods until 23 Feb. ⚡

# EXECUTIVE REMOTE POSITIONS

Are you a global travel nomad or want to be part of the work from anywhere club? Well, the good news is you can as an executive! Ironically, part of the trail was blazed by the pandemic when office workers transitioned to working from home.

In my practice, the number of clients seeking remote positions as a CIO (chief information officer), CPO (chief product officer) or CMO (chief marketing officer) is growing. In March 2021, Statista conducted a study of 1,200 CIOs and found that 70% of respondents worked remotely, and these CIOs believed permanent remote work would increase post-pandemic.[1]

Remote working is not a new concept for Fortune companies. Over 15 years ago, the team I led at Sprint comprised those working from home, whether in Kansas City, the Washington, D.C., area or Dallas. As a manager, I discussed with individuals whether it was a good fit to work remotely. A few team members desired to permanently work remotely, while others enjoyed being in the office for the camaraderie or potential to avoid distractions at home. In total, the majority, including myself, worked from home one day per week. I did not observe any negative impacts, while some of my peers forbade the practice of working from home. And, keep in mind, we all worked for the same company. My perspective is: hire competent people, observe their productivity, and, if an issue pops up, have a conversation to find a resolution. Guess what? I never rescinded the remote working flexibility.

In this chapter exploring **Executive Remote Positions**, I will discuss how to:

- find resources for remote job opportunities,
- evaluate personal and professional considerations, and
- work from another continent.

In my memory, there has never been a better time to work outside a corporate office. It is more widely accepted, and companies, mostly, have pivoted, including the FAANG (Facebook, Amazon, Apple, Netflix, and Google) companies.

According to a 2020 survey of large North American employers, companies expect that their full-time employees working from home will level off at around 19% from the pandemic crisis peak of almost 100%.[2]

## EVALUATING PERSONAL & PROFESSIONAL CONSIDERATIONS

It might sound glamorous to work from anywhere. You should consider the following items if you desire a remote position, whether the employer pays you to, or you opt to take this route on your own initiative.

- **Leadership Visibility**: Out of sight might mean out of mind for promotions. Scenario: My client Mike established and led the first overseas software development center in India for a logistics company based in Seattle. Within 36 months, he interviewed, hired, and onboarded 100 colleagues, including 10 direct managers. Being a continent away for four years in an unfamiliar environment, he confided he felt isolated from his family during those years, especially since his son was born in India. Further, he was not in the hallways taking part in person with the executive leadership team back at the headquarters. His boss promised Mike a promotion when he came back from India; unfortunately, this did not transpire immediately. It took another 19 months before Mike attained his desired director role.
- **Taxes**: If you are a permanent resident of the U.S. and you work remotely outside of the country, you may be subjected to the tax laws of that country. If you are visiting for a limited time, you should be able to work remotely legally without any issues. The IRS

has an interactive tax assistant for foreign-earned income exclusions on the U.S. federal tax return. It is best to refer to your company's HR department and a tax expert to understand the financial ramifications.

- **Company Policy**: What are your company's remote employee guidelines? Some employers allow employees flexibility in where they live, while others dictate the workforce location. It might not even be up to a company but rather the country's requirements for work visas, taxes, or certifications. The same goes if you are testing what it is like to work abroad. You have a vested interest in determining your company policy.

## WORKING FROM ANOTHER CONTINENT

You might think it complicated to set up your remote workplace, whether as a consultant or employee not supported by headquarters. It is not.

My husband and I spend, on average, two months a year outside the U.S. living in Europe, the Caribbean, or South America as part of our global travel bucket list. So much has changed in technology within the past 20 years since we have been traveling together. Now you can vet so many aspects of global travel online as an individual traveler for working anywhere with a data connection. Since I still consult while traveling abroad, here are five items I believe are mandatory for a suitable work environment.

- **Lodging**: The options to review and book accommodations are a couple of clicks away. In Europe, Airbnb or an in-country region-specific lodging website offers the best selection of accommodations. What is great about using these sites is that you can access photos, read past guests reviews, and select specific features such as Wi-Fi, air conditioning, and washing machine while pinpointing on the city map your desired location. Plus, for payment, you can pay in dollars or local currency online with your credit card, to help amass frequent flyer award miles. For Costa del Sol in Spain, I recommend Solaga. I have used VRBO, but I find it provides fewer available listings in Europe compared to the U.S. Another option is using Booking.com, which provides a travel meta-search engine for lodging reservations, featuring apartments, hostels, and hotels. In the past five years, we have operated this way for one-month stays in Bordeaux, Buenos Aires, Gran Canaria, Malaga, Palermo, Sitges, Split, and St. Maarten without a problem with payment or accommodation access.

- **Supplemental Medical Insurance**: Since we live outside the U.S. for a couple of months each year, I purchase online supplemental medical insurance. I have United Healthcare, and Pat has Medicare. I bought a supplement through SafeTrip UnitedHealthcare Global. Why? Health insurance policies, including Medicare policies, which are valid where you live in the U.S., rarely include medical coverage or evacuation coverage when abroad. The SafeTrip supplement allows most physicians and hospitals to provide you with the necessary medical treatment while abroad. It will either send their bill directly to UnitedHealthcare Global or, in the case of small dollar amounts, may ask you to pay at the time services are rendered. Think of them as your medical concierge at a great value price of approximately $660 annually (based on 2021 rates), covering me for up to $500,000 in medical services with a $250 deductible with lesser coverage for my husband due to age. You can call them 24 hours a day, 7 days a week, and 365 days a year for assistance with medical and travel, including the replacement of lost or stolen travel documents and emergency travel arrangements. Think it can't happen to you? It can. I fell in Spain when hiking down a hilltop, nothing major that Advil and ice packs could not fix. On the other hand, I had a friend who had to be evacuated from Fiji to Los Angeles for emergency surgery. This type of service made all the travel arrangements and paid for her husband's 1-week hotel stay while out of state from Austin.

- **Wireless Phone**: My husband and I signed up for Google Fi phone service in 2019 and save a bundle in the U.S. and abroad. It is a sizable difference with no need to call the wireless provider to let them know you are traveling to over 200 global destinations available with Google Fi. While in Spain, calls were 20 cents/minute, data was $10/GB, and the text was unlimited on our $35 monthly phone plan for two users. That is not a typo. Yes, you can BYOD (bring your own device) such as a phone from Costco. Our August 2021 usage bill covering both of us, including voice, data, text, and taxes, was only $52.15, while the previous month was only $54.65. Plus, it provides voicemail to text free-of-charge. We had Wi-Fi in our apartment rental, so there was no data usage except when we ventured out for directions to the incredible restaurants and sightseeing locations. By comparison, when we lived in Bordeaux, France, for a month, we signed up for the international Verizon Wireless plan. It charged $40 per line monthly for 100 talk minutes, 100 text, and 100 MB data, and that was on top of my regular monthly rate, which for two people was over $100 monthly. I, unfortunately, used my Pandora for a daily walk and racked up $25/100 MB in overcharges. In short order, we turned our phones off except for directions, making reservations, or an unplanned emergency. Other cost-effective options to consider include international SIM cards, rentable global phones delivered before your trip, and a mobile phone app called WhatsApp that downloads to your Android or iPhone for calling and texting.

WhatsApp voice and video calls use your
phone's Internet connection instead of your
cell plan's voice minutes, so you don't have
to worry about expensive calling charges.

- **Wi-Fi Connection**: When my husband
and I travel, we bring our computers and
iPads. Three years ago, in Palermo, Sicily,
the apartment listing offered Internet but
not the details of connection speed nor
usage; therefore, we were surprised by the 1
MB speed and prepaid 40 GB monthly
capped data plan. After days of frustration,
I learned to ask rental owners for the
details. The apartment in Palermo was built
into the fortified Aragonese Wall
constructed in the 1500s by the Spanish
administration, which was more than 3 feet
thick but luckily had windows. The router
had to be placed in a window for best signal
access. The slow speed created video
transmission pixilation issues, plus whoever
was using their device first had a better
video quality. After streaming Netflix for
two days on two devices, our data usage
allocation was depleted for €32,80. The
apartment rental owner chided us, which
made me look for alternatives. The solution
was ordering a pocket Wi Tourist wi-fi
router that was shipped to me in three
business days from Milan. It provided 3G
and 4G access options, 150 MB
download/50 MB upload speeds, unlimited
data usage, and over 1,200 rental locations
to drop off the unit for return after our

month's stay in prepaid return packaging. The cost back then was €3,70 /day with a small deposit of €35. Brilliant.

- **Universal Power Adapter**: Purchasing one of these is critical for connecting your phone, computer, and other rechargeable devices. We purchased a country-compatible wall plug by Bestek through Amazon, which offers two electrical sockets and five USB ports for our wireless world. For around $40, we have power access in Australia and the EU with a universal travel adapter 220V to 110V voltage converter and a worldwide plug adapter. The only issue is that it takes up weight and space in your luggage, so look at its dimensions. Or have your significant other pack it, which is my solution since I purchase items to bring back home.

If you are ready to pack your bags, it is time for the next exercise. If not, you can skip to the next chapter for C-Suite advice.

## EXERCISE: PUT IT INTO PRACTICE

If remote roles pique your interest, let's walk through action items to get you started. Please go to the worksheet for **Roadmap #1: Remote Executive Positions** to complete the exercise below.

### Action Plan

Did you know you could curate remote positions? From networking to job search tools, you have several options. Below are ideas to kick start your remote quest.

1. **Executive Recruiter:** Most executives network or have search companies contact them. It is ideal for nurturing contacts to become a virtual CxO. I have two clients currently in remote executive roles. In fact, their entire leadership team is not located in a traditional headquarters.

> a)   Contact your recruiter to focus on remote roles. If you do not have a recruiter, ask a colleague or search for one online. With $2 billion in revenue, Korn Ferry is the world's leading executive search firm. You can sign up to their website and browse for opportunities free-of-charge. Keep in mind that executive search firms work for the hiring company, not you.

2. **LinkedIn:** When I checked in August 2021, more than 2,000 job postings were listed within the U.S. for remote roles requiring executive experience. Below are the following steps on LinkedIn.

> a)   Access the "Job" tab. In "Search for your next job," after entering your dream job title, enter "remote" in the "city/state/zip" field.
> b)   Save that search as a "job alert." Now remote jobs will be sent to your email at the frequency you selected.

3. **ExecThread Platform:** In 2021, I became aware of this platform that shares job executive opportuni-

ties. ExecThread crowdsources thousands of executive job opportunities from members who anonymously share positions they know about but do not plan to pursue. It is free to join, or you can sign up for a monthly subscription to obtain job description detail.

4. **Create a Remote Role:** Just because a position is in a particular city does not mean you have to work there, especially in today's environment. Be armed with the rationale for staying put and create a positioning statement regarding benefits to the company of you working remotely, i.e., what is in it for them? Develop four concrete reasons.

a)   Statistics: You can cite research statistics for your industry.
b)   Experience: Highlight your career experience managing remote teams across the U.S. or the globe.
c)   Savings: Explain that they will save on corporate relocation expenses.
d)   References: Obtain former leadership recommendations on your virtual prowess.

## KEY TAKEAWAYS

In this chapter exploring **Executive Remote Positions**, you learned about:

- finding resources for remote job opportunities,
- evaluating personal and professional considerations, and

- working from another continent.

With a remote mindset, you can join the ranks of the CEO, CPO, and CTO in my practice who work in Austin and Seattle while the rest of their executive team lives elsewhere. Although there are fewer opportunities within Fortune 2000, the startup environment appears to embrace this operating model.

Congratulations on completing your first roadmap point! In this section of four chapters, you have read about the merits for:

- developing your career vision,
- confronting indecision,
- evaluating corporate versus startup roles, and
- considering remote executive positions.

Are you ready to hang out in the C-Suite? In the next section, we arrive at the second roadmap point. I will cover thinking like a CEO, finding mentors and coaches, investing in yourself, and joining a board of directors.

# Career Roadmap Point #2
## C-Suite Advice

Since we wrapped up the first part of your 5-step roadmap, it is time to get insight from the **C-Suite**. If you desire to become a chief executive, there is minimal seating at the table. It is no secret I am enamored by research statistics, especially when they provide fascinating revelations regarding the probability of joining the executive ranks.

The U.S. Bureau of Labor Statistics estimates that only 200,000 individuals are employed as chief executives in the U.S.; location-wise, over 1/3 of them work in California, Florida, Illinois, New York, and Tennessee.[1] The latest U.S. Census Bureau claims almost 8 million employer establishments exist.[2] Net, to increase your probability of becoming a chief executive, you need to laser focus on where you want to live, and you need to network with individuals sitting in the C-Suite.

And for the C-Suite, it encompasses the executives at the top level of the company pyramid based upon oversight and scope, typically as a CEO, CFO, COO, CTO, and CMO. Within the past decade, I observed a trend toward creating niche executive roles like a Chief Sustainability Officer, Chief Experience Officer, Chief Data Officer, Chief Accessibility Officer, and Chief Diversity Officer.

Chief executive titles may differ from established corporations to startups, and then you need to consider global location variances. Here is the catch: C-Suite titles do not always begin with the letter C. For example, there are cases whereby a VP of Operations is considered a higher-ranking employee compared to a COO. Plus, for some companies, the most elevated role is President.

The reason clients show up at my virtual doorstep is that they desire a new executive role. Depending on their background, they seek a specific title ranging from Director to Partner to General Manager, not just the C-Suite.

Whatever they are called, the C-Suite's mission is to collaborate, ensuring the company's strategies and operations align to drive profitable customer solutions. I recall from my annual Sprint performance reviews a focus on four key factors: increasing profitability, reducing operating expenses, augmenting customer satisfaction, and addressing employee satisfaction. My challenge was that Sprint ranked employees last on the list, while I believe employees should be first since, in my experience, happy campers drive the other three corporate results.

At this second roadmap point for **C-Suite Advice**, I will share research based upon best practices and client observations to:

- think like a CEO,
- benefit from mentor and coach collaborations,
- invest in your continuing education, and
- join boards and professional associations for networking opportunities and social impact.

# THINK LIKE A CEO

While not everyone aspires to become a CEO, it is important if you manage teams to have a benchmark for leadership to identify your top skills. These leadership characteristics are to be highlighted on your resume, LinkedIn profile, and discussed during job interviews. I researched characteristics and admirable qualities.

*Fortune Magazine* conducts an annual survey amongst Fortune 500 CEOs. One question is which Fortune 500 CEO—other than themselves—they most admire. Below are the April 2020 results occurring, coincidentally, just at the beginning of the pandemic.[1]

- JPMorgan: Jamie Dimon 23%
- Walmart: Doug McMillon 16%
- Microsoft: Satya Nadella 7%
- Amazon: Jeff Bezos 7%

- Received over one vote from a CEO peer:
  Salesforce's Marc Benioff, GE's Larry Culp,
  Mastercard's Ajay Banga, J&J's Alex Gorsky,
  Apple's Tim Cook, and Berkshire
  Hathaway's Warren Buffett

One of my clients is a fan of Jamie Dimon related to his business acumen for driving incremental revenue, especially during the 2020 pandemic. Furthermore, my client admires Jamie's candid and forthright communication, including taking ownership for failures. During a 2017 sit-down interview attended by Stanford University Graduate School of Business students, the moderator asked Jamie what leadership qualities he looks for in people in their 20s.

Jamie remarked that young adults gain authentic leadership with career and life experience. He appreciates three qualities in anyone of any age. First, he values subject matter experts because they enhance your knowledge base with information. Second, your character is a sine qua non, meaning Jamie appreciates a person who can tell the whole truth, nothing but the truth, and does not shave the truth. Third, he gravitates toward people that relate well with others. In summary, you would be in Jamie's consideration set if you are a collaborative domain specialist with integrity.

As a counter to my client regarding the most admired Fortune 500 CEO, I am a Doug McMillon enthusiast since I have financially benefited as a Walmart stockholder receiving continuous annual return rates. I am impressed that Walmart remarkably hired 400,000 people as a part of its 2.45 million worldwide employee base during the Covid crisis. While other companies froze recruitment during this tumultuous period or unfortunately went out of business, Walmart brought hundreds of thousands of households a paycheck. .

In this chapter uncovering how to **Think Like a CEO**, I will:

- review C-Suite leadership research,
- identify top CEO characteristics, and
- discover your highest-ranking soft and hard skills.

## C-SUITE LEADERSHIP RESEARCH

If you are in a leadership position or desire to climb the corporate ladder, what things should you consider? The 10-year CEO Genome Project of 2,600 leaders revealed four surprising results on CEO ascensions:[2]

- over 70% became CEO after years in their career
- 45% of candidates had career blowups
- 8% did not graduate from college
- 7% did not attend an Ivy League school

Within the same study, CEOs shared similar traits that anyone can master: being decisive, relentlessly reliable, boldly adapting, and engaging with stakeholders without shying away from conflict. This research result fits JPMorgan's Jamie Dimon to a tee.

Sam Reese is the CEO of Vistage, one of the world's largest CEO coaching and peer advisory organizations for small and midsize businesses. In a business journal article, he shared an evolution in CEO qualities and how leaders think about their companies, employees, communities, and even themselves. Sam believes that leaders set the conditions for success in eight ways:[3]

- Your purpose is fuel
- Drive the culture you believe in
- Bridge the generational divide
- Champion candor and transparency
- Embrace vulnerability as a strength
- Know the details of your business, but don't get stuck in the weeds
- Challenge your perspective
- Make a decision

Sam's thought process reminds me of my first session with Imran, a CTO trailblazer in AgTech, when we talked about his brand image.

I asked him, "Tell me about yourself in three concise sentences. Only think about the past 10 years."

Imran thought for a moment and said, "I am a results-oriented leader."

When I explained that for an executive recruiter interview it is necessary to tie it into a specific domain, he said, "It does not matter what you give me. It can be bioinformatics or building a data architecture for a company; I empower and enable staff to be successful. As a visionary, I lead the team with a clear strategy to achieve that vision."

Focusing on his team, he explained, "I currently have 45 full-time employees and 20 contractors across the globe. I have a startup mindset. I build high-performing teams and an organization from the ground up."

When I asked about how he built teams, he responded, "I give them core values such as transparency and dedication. They, in turn, come up with ways to interact with one another. It is important for them to share, be vulnerable, and build trust."

Imran's success differentiator as a tech executive is his high EQ (emotional quotient) combined with a Ph.D. in bioinformatics, an MBA, and an MS in biotechnology. He is the poster child for the 2019 Gartner TalentNeuron research. The study reveals that C-Suite executives must have technical skills such as advanced-tech knowledge, besides design thinking soft skills.[4] Gartner's top 10 emerging soft skills covering cognition and social aspects derive from the analysis of 400 job postings:

- Adaptability
- Complaint management
- Customer relations
- Customer satisfaction
- Data governance
- Demand planning
- Design thinking
- Sales leadership
- Sales skills

- Strategic management

I am enlightened on what Gartner considers a soft skill. Data governance and demand planning?

## DISCOVERING YOUR TOP SKILLS

As previously mentioned, talking about yourself is challenging for most job search candidates. How do you respond to, "So, tell me about yourself"? I bet it depends on your audience and situation. At a neighborhood get-together, it is a simple "I'm an engineering director at Microsoft." Full stop. While with a recruiter, it might be a deer in the headlights moment. "I'm an engineering director with 250 direct reports with responsibility for Azure initiatives related to accessibility."

> "Your brand is what other people say about you when you're not in the room."
>
> — JEFF BEZOS, FORMER CEO, AMAZON

You have 30 seconds to make an excellent first impression, but how? In my consulting practice, we start with the basics, your skills. What you bring to the table and how to differentiate yourself from the other top three candidates vying for the same position is personal branding 101.

Since seeking employment is not a routine occurrence, clients are often challenged when I ask them to list their top 10 skills.

I simplify this process by conducting a skills mapping across three job listings of their choice. Then, I create a spreadsheet with the skills sourced from their LinkedIn profile, three job listings, brainstorming, and people they admire. Over half the time, what clients ranked as crucial skills during our initial discussions do not show up on the job postings the client selected. Unfortunately, the client's top skills were not relevant to a hiring company. I change a client's mindset by stating we need to address the company's top skills in their resume, LinkedIn profile, and elevator pitch. Why would they hire you?

Developing your brand by highlighting your skills is critical to your career advancement. Evaluating and prioritizing your skills will help set the stage for success.

## EXERCISE: PUT IT INTO PRACTICE

Please go to your worksheet for **Roadmap #2: Think Like a CEO** to conduct your skills assessment.

**Action Plan**

While working with clients, as I mentioned, I create a skills map for their next career adventure. My client intake questionnaire has an exercise to list your top five soft skills related to leadership, plus the top five hard skills for industry expertise. You can do the same derived from the resources shown below.

1. **LinkedIn Profile:** Thirteen years ago, upon opening the LinkedIn app, a select number of network connections would appear at the top of my profile page. The LinkedIn app, versus my business colleague, had created an automated question regarding whether I wanted to endorse a particular individual for specific skills. I refer to this as the crowdsourcing of your skills. While some skills appearing on your profile are perplexing, this is a good start for cultivating a baseline for your top skill sets. On your LinkedIn profile are three major skill categories regarding your industry knowledge, tools and technology, and interpersonal abilities.

2. **Job Postings:** I ask clients to provide three job listings related to their dream job. From that, I highlight the job description keywords related to responsibilities and minimum requirements. My clients are attracted to these positions because they believe their skill set matches. Sometimes they might be a perfect match for a job;

other times, some clients misunderstand the industry terminology or, unfortunately, are in denial. If your resume and/or LinkedIn profile do not match over 50%, the recruiter probably will not be contacting you.

3. **Brainstorming:** During our sessions, I ask clients to explain how others describe them. It is intriguing the adjectives their significant others and colleagues use. I asked a colleague that question about myself. He stated that my top four qualities for being a career consultant were attention to detail, broad knowledge of the tech marketplace, subject matter knowledge of job placement strategies, and that I am an enthusiastic cheerleader. Some of these attributes I did not think about, but he did. What are you missing out on in your skills inventory that a potential recruiter or hiring manager is seeking? Most technologists describe themselves in terms of, you guessed it, technical expertise such as Agile, Lean Six Sigma, Cloud Computing, Cybersecurity, and Program Management. For executives, it is undoubtedly important to have a tech background, but the research points out leadership qualities are just as important. Are you a cross-functional collaborator, industry thought leader, or influencer? These are highly desirable soft skills.

4. **People You Admire:** When I am developing brands for clients, I search for the best Engineering VP or CTO LinkedIn

profiles as examples of current industry positioning. At the height of their game, you can pick up leadership characteristics from their LinkedIn bios, presentations, or interviews. These executives have hit the apex of their careers based on presentation skills, innovative processes, or treatment of employees, I endorse cloning and owning their best traits and matching them up with your skill differentiators.

Below is a partial list of what I developed for Imran based upon his LinkedIn CTO profile and analysis of the four job postings he provided.

**Industry Expertise** (hard skills)

- Agile certified
- Architectures
- Cloud computing
- Compliance
- Computer science
- Continuous improvement
- Data analysis
- Data science & data engineering
- Data warehousing
- Distributed Systems
- Enterprise solution
- Information Technology (IT)
- Machine Learning
- Product development
- Portfolio management
- SaaS
- Security

- Software Development Life Cycle


**Leadership** (soft skills)

- Building high-performance teams
- Business acumen
- Business operations
- Business strategy
- Collaborative problem solving
- Conflict management
- Cross-functional team leadership
- Cultural diversity
- Emotional Intelligence
- Innovation
- Integrity
- Negotiation
- Organizational development
- Partnership development
- Strategic planning
- Thought leadership
- Vendor management
- Vision


## KEY TAKEAWAYS

In this chapter on how to **Think Like a CEO**, you learned about:

- reviewing C-Suite leadership research,
- identifying top CEO characteristics, and
- discovering your highest-ranking soft and hard skills.

If you are decisive, relentlessly reliable, boldly adaptive, and engaging with stakeholders without shying away from conflict, you passed the CEO thinking test. And JPMorgan's Jamie Dimon might want to hang out with you.

If you lack specific leadership skills, I encourage you to seek help, whether from reading leadership books, attending executive courses, finding a mentor, or hiring a coach.

Thinking about help, this is an excellent segue to the next chapter, where I will discuss the importance of having a mentor or a career coach.

# MENTORS & COACHES

Clients seek my counsel for personal brand image positioning, including resumes and LinkedIn profile optimization. There is another piece to the puzzle for career enhancement engaging with a mentor.

The University of Washington defines the role of a mentor:

> "A mentor may share with a mentee (or protege) information about his or her own career path, as well as provide guidance, motivation, emotional support, and role modeling. A mentor may help with exploring careers, setting goals, developing contacts, and identifying resources."[1]

While researching this topic, I came across this article about tech CEOs and their mentors written by Alex Bracetti, a contributing writer for Complex

Media.[2] He shares that most of the FAANG entrepreneurs had one or more mentors.

- **Apple**: Steve Jobs's mentor was Andy Groves, the co-founder of Intel
- **Facebook**: Mark Zuckerberg's mentor was Don Graham, the CEO of the *Washington Post*
- **Foursquare**: Dennis Crowley's mentor was Ken Allard, his former boss at Juniper Communications
- **Google**: Larry Page's mentor was Michael Bloomberg
- **Yahoo**: Marissa Mayer's mentor was Larry Page

Any surprises here for you? There were a couple for me.

In this chapter, we will focus on the merits of **Mentors & Coaches** for how to:

- gain a better understanding of how they can support your efforts,
- determine resources to find one that fits your needs, and
- establish the ground rules for optimizing your time with them.

## FINDING YOUR MENTOR

If you have determined you need mentoring guidance, where do you go? There is a supply-demand imbalance, according to Rick Woolworth. He notes in a *Harvard Business Review* article that while over 75% of professionals desire a mentor, unfortunately, only 37% have one.[3] It made me think mentor demand with a lack of supply equals an excellent opportunity for a startup; I searched online. There are options out there to either pay for a mentor or access free resources.

I compiled a list for the unpaid route to find your trusted advisor without the startup subscription model fee.

- **Former Bosses or Colleagues**: Have you worked with someone you admire who went on and attained the ultimate role you desire? Reach out to them, tell them you want to meet for coffee or tea, and then catch up. If you feel connected, seize the opportunity to ask them to become your mentor. An alternative is to ask them for potential mentors that can provide constructive feedback.
- **Current Senior Management**: Find someone with a common interest within your current company that you believe could lend you support. If they have the capacity, they would be flattered to support a co-worker. If not, they are not your people, so contact someone else.
- **Professional Associations**: Most professional associations have monthly meetings and annual conferences. These are the perfect venues to meet like-minded professionals with experience that could

benefit your new venture or career journey. I joined the WomenTech Network and the International Coaching Federation, which offer mentoring opportunities for members. I was delighted when WomenTech Network CEO and Founder Anna Radulovski reached out to me in July 2021 to say I was selected to be a mentor for the August cohort.

- **Industry Meetups**: You can search an Industry Meetups site to find local events to attend. For example, I found a Seattle tech mentoring event on Capitol Hill free-of-charge. Similar events can be found globally.

- **Social Media**: I follow CEOs and entrepreneurs across various fields, from technology to career consulting. They offer expert advice through their blogs, newsletters, Instagram, and LinkedIn accounts. Consider these virtual mentors or take the next step and set up a call. This year I reached out to two dozen people I admire across the globe. What is great about virtual connections is you do not need to be geographically near a mentor. Similarly, I have had 10 people reach out to me in the past year for my expertise. LinkedIn has terrific groups, along with Instagram and Twitter. My advice is to get involved by following a career-related hashtag (e.g., #careers #careeradvice #jobsearch #mentoring #branding #personaldevelopment).

- **Friends & Family**: Last but not least, ask

your personal friends for suggestions. As you would ask friends for advice related to a repair or medical professional, do the same for finding a mentor. Sometimes your mentor might sit across from you at the breakfast table. In my case, my husband has been a great mentor for my former enterprise sales role since he was an executive with over 20 years of sales success.

## MEETING OPTIMIZATION

What is the best way to set up a mentoring session? It is as simple as coordinating schedules for a 30-minute to 1-hour meeting at the convenience of your new advisor. Best practices include having a prepared agenda for what you want to accomplish in your limited time frame.

According to Effectiviology, a website focused on applying psychology and philosophy to practical applications, "Writing notes by hand generally improves your understanding of the material and helps you remember it better, since writing it down involves deeper cognitive-processing of the material than typing it."[4]

I recommend using this approach while taking notes in a journal during your mentoring session without the distraction of the technology of your phone, computer, or iPad. Close the meeting with the next steps, action items, and schedule your following session. Mentoring is a monthly or quarterly initiative, while coaching varies from weekly to monthly.

These conversations can take place in person, via video, or by phone.

Send your new mentor a thank you note. For content, reiterate what you are striving for in the mentoring relationship.

As a mentor at Dress for Success and WomenTech Network, the relationships, collaborations, and successes shared during updates are uplifting. It is a win-win.

Now that we have covered the merits of having a mentor, let's see if it makes sense for you to hire a coach.

## DO YOU NEED A CAREER COACH?

Obtaining an outside perspective is helpful when focusing on your career trajectory. If you are unsure on the path to take or need assistance with your positioning, interviewing, resume development, or LinkedIn, a career coach closes the gap.

There are different types of career coaching styles.

Some coaches will provide guidance to assess your career interests, grow your leadership presence, and establish a work-life balance with you doing all the work. Other coaches are job positioning experts who create search strategies and develop tools such as resumes and LinkedIn optimizations. A minority of coaches do both.

As with finding mentors, there are many ways to locate a career coach. My recommendation is to check with colleagues and friends initially. LinkedIn is an alternative resource.

As of October 2021, LinkedIn has 1,010,000 people identifying themselves as a "career coach" as a job title. Here is the kicker: anyone can call themselves a career coach. According to the 2020 report published by the International Coaching Federation (ICF) in partnership with PricewaterhouseCoopers (PwC), there are 71,000 certified coach practitioners worldwide, which equates to less than 10% of the LinkedIn self-professors.[5] The best bet is to assess an individual's credentials and recommendations, as you would for any other paid service.

LinkedIn Profinder is one avenue you can try to find a career coach.

Per their website: "Review Trusted LinkedIn Experts & Choose the Skills You Need. Top Freelance Talent. Local Professionals." Based on your LinkedIn profile location, for no initial charge, you can submit a career coach request and receive five proposals to work with someone within your geographic area. The service options for hiring a professional career advocate include:

- Create a 60-day plan or 360-view
- Tactics on navigating an organization's processes and politics
- Managing work and life priorities
- Developing a strategy to grow your leadership presence

To explain the benefits of the career coaching process, I offer an analogy. Do you know that junk drawer in your kitchen or office? Amazing, I knew you had one. The sad fact is that we all do. I help my executive clients clean up their career junk drawer so they can clinch their next role.

Oliver, a former executive in charge of music partner integration, summed it up best during our initial phone consult: "You are the Marie Kondo for job search strategy."

I was flattered yet vaguely unfamiliar with Marie, so I simply said, "Great!"

As soon as the call was over, I googled "Marie Kondo." It turns out Marie has a cult-like following as a Japanese organizing consultant, author, and TV show host. Known as Konmari to fans, she has written four books on organizing, which have collectively sold millions of copies worldwide. It appears Marie and I have four things in common—we are organizational fiends, identify as female, share the same first initial, and are book authors. We diverge in terms of focus; I'm focused on your career strategy while she focuses on your home's junk drawer.

The *Harvard Business Review* surveyed 140 leading coaches and invited five experts to comment on the findings.[6] The top three reasons clients engage executive coaches are:

- 48% develop high potential or facilitate a transition
- 26% act as a sounding board

- 12% address derailing behavior

Further, the magazine article mentioned, "The right match is absolutely key to the success of a coaching experience. Without it, the trust required for optimal executive performance will not develop."

In my initial consultation call, I state that if we are not a match, why work together? I curate clientele collaborations for successful outcomes.

I first became familiar with executive coaches when I worked at Sprint. Not that I had one, but the executives I reported to did, and these were highly regarded internal corporate coaches. As mentioned in the book introduction, I initially volunteered as a career coach and then pivoted to becoming an executive career coach. Right before Covid in February 2020, I decided to become a certified coach. As a lifelong learner, I invested in a 6-month course from the Colorado-based Coach Training Alliance and successfully passed my certification exam in the fall of 2020.

My coaching cohort comprised 10 individuals hailing from Canada, Egypt, Italy, Saudi Arabia, and the U.S. We participated in weekly calls, conducted over 30 in-class coaching sessions, read a 468-page textbook, and completed 1-4 hours of weekly homework. In parallel with my practice, I spent 20 hours per week coaching executive clients and not-for-profit Dress for Success clients.

I have been a tech executive career consultant and volunteer career advocate at Dress for Success in Austin and Seattle for more than four years. I enjoy helping people find their career True North. By attaining the executive career coach certification, I hope to offer more value to my clients as an account-ability partner.

## MY CLIENTS

My clients come from intriguing backgrounds around the globe. It is a melting pot of clients from Africa, Australia, Bosnia, China, India, Israel, Peru, Romania, Slovenia, Taiwan, U.K., Ukraine, Vietnam, and the U.S. It is truly fascinating to learn from those not born in the U.S. about their childhood and what brought them here.

Their executive titles are an alphabet soup: CEO, CIO, CISO, CMO, COO, CPO, CRO, CSO, CTO, GM, and VP. Then there are presidents, directors, managers, and heads of groups aspiring to the next step in their career.

For my volunteering, I coach primarily outside of tech. I meet fashionistas, women waiting on work visas, new college graduates, formerly incarcerated individuals, and women returning to the workforce after raising children. I enjoy our discussions since everyone has a passion for making a significant impact. It is the common thread. Not money, not title, merely making a difference and leaving a legacy.

I learn something new every time I coach or consult with a client. It reminds me you should do what you love.

## EXERCISE: PUT IT INTO PRACTICE

Please go to your worksheet for **Roadmap #2: Mentors & Coaches** and fill out the action plan.

**Action Plan**

1. Reach out to colleagues for mentor or coach recommendations

2. Identify 3 potential mentors

3. Identify coaching sources

    a) Professional association
    b) Meetup group
    c) Google search
    d) Other

4. LinkedIn Pro

    a) Create coaching request & submit
    b) Review 5 proposals
    c) Set up a call with 1-3 coaches to review services and pricing
    d) Establish your initial meeting

## KEY TAKEAWAYS

In this chapter covering the difference between a **Mentor & Coach**, you learned about:

- gaining a better understanding of how they can support your efforts,

- determining resources to find a one that fits
  your needs, and
- establishing ground rules for optimizing
  your time with them.

Over the years, I met with several mentors for different career aspects. Typically, they have been bosses; in recent years, colleagues in niche roles fill the mentor role. A standout was my first boss, who introduced me to the world of global consulting. On my author journey, I turned to fellow writers for book publishing tips.

If you do not have a mentor, it is time to reach out. While you are at it, see if a coach could support your endeavors.

In the next chapter, we will explore advanced learning to further your career.

# INVESTING IN YOURSELF

I might be the odd kid, but I was not too fond of summer breaks in elementary school because I could not attend and learn new things. I was listless, telling my mom I was bored; in turn, she would assign mundane chores like polishing silver or dusting furniture. As mentioned within the first chapter, I am a first-generation American of European parents, so Mom taught me what my husband refers to as Dutch cleaning skills. My mom's cleaning training was free of charge; in fact, she paid me a weekly allowance. In today's job vernacular, it was a paid child internship. As a quick learner, I quit saying I was bored and lost myself in the world of literature. I would check out the maximum weekly allotment of library books and referenced our set of Encyclopedia Britannica to learn weird facts. For some reason, we ended up with two sets of Britannica. For anyone born after 1980, you probably have no clue what I'm talking about. No matter, please read on.

## HARD COPY EDITION OF WIKIPEDIA

If you are not familiar with the Encyclopedia Britannica—you cannot say one word without the other—it is the written form of Wikipedia sold in the 1960s-70s by in-person salespeople. It was an era when door-to-door soliciting was embraced. Why? Because there was no Internet, streaming, or iPhones to compete with someone showing up at your front doorstep. People read printed books back then; how things have evolved with the Amazon Kindle.

I was curious if the e-reader phenomena might have eroded printed book sales. Statista contends that over 650 million printed books are sold annually in the U.S., with more than 65% of adults having read a print book in the past 12 months.[1]

Here is the intriguing fact about the Encyclopedia Britannica: their printing press published these volumes for a mind-boggling 244 years. I loved it as a reference tool for papers and projects from elementary through high school. It was worldly knowledge—I'm sure skewed with the printed fake news of the day—with a complete set of a dozen or more hardbound volumes covering topics from "Astronomy" to "Zoology" in my home library. It was my learning nirvana. Today you'd probably just stack a couple of volumes on their side for the best framed Zoom session or Instagram selfie.

According to Wikipedia, Encyclopedia Britannica "was written by about 100 full-time editors and over 4,000 contributors. The 2010 version of the 15th edition, which spans 32 volumes and 32,640 pages, was the last printed edition."[2]

When my mother passed away a few years ago, I wanted to keep a childhood Britannica set and then wondered where I would put it in our condo without built-in shelves. Side note: built-ins are part of next year's condo renovation budget. I see a Britannica set purchased in the future from Half Price Books.

In this chapter for **Investing in Yourself**, I will be:

- sharing different learning styles,
- observing the benefits of continuous adult education, and
- highlighting potential advanced degrees and technical certifications.

Learning is ongoing throughout one's life. It does not end with your high school or college degree. There are industry certifications, corporate training courses, and life lessons, including the school of hard knocks. I tell my clients to embrace it. If you desire an alternative career path, then I advise taking a class or a seminar.

Even those of us from Britannica age go on a learning rampage. In the past two years, I took an arduous Tai Chi class (failed), a fabulous cupcake with champagne appreciation course (indulged), and a challenging 4-month group tutoring classes for languages including Italian and French (focused). My French is still abysmal, but I could count, find opening hours and days, and be courteous while spending two months in Bordeaux and St. Maarten.

To prepare for a month abroad living in Malaga, Spain, I attended a 2-month course at City University in Seattle to refresh my high school Spanish. It was an immersion class with no English spoken. This class was my opportunity to ramp up my Spanish skills and meet fellow learning adventurers. In preparation for writing this book, I took a 10-week writing course in the Spring of 2021.

As it turns out, we don't all have similar learning styles.

## INDUSTRY RESEARCH LEARNING STYLES

A Pew Research Center survey several years ago revealed how, as ongoing learners, people fall into three self-described categories:[3]

- 74% of adults are **personal learners**—they have taken part in at least one of several activities in the past 12 months to advance their knowledge about something that interests them. These activities include reading, taking courses, or attending meetings or events tied to learning more about their personal interests.
- 73% of adults consider themselves **lifelong learners**.
- 63% of those working (or 36% of all adults) are **professional learners**. They have taken a course or gotten additional training in the past 12 months to improve their job skills or expertise connected to career advancement.

How would you describe yourself: personal, lifelong, or professional learner?

## ADULT CONTINUED EDUCATION BENEFITS

As a career consultant, I receive dozens of requests daily via LinkedIn Pro for career coaching, resume help, LinkedIn makeovers, and job interview preparation. Before taking on a prospective client, I review their accomplishments, including credentials and academics. There are rock stars and clients needing a discussion about how to up their game. One answer to gain recruiting prominence is adding credibility with education. I believe there are four benefits to professional learning:

- **Keeps you current**: Technology has leapfrogged in the past five years, so take on the personal cost of an AWS, Azure, Cisco, Google, or VMware certification if your company will not pay for it. If you want a $25,000 pay increase or job title advancement, what is a $200-$2,000 out-of-pocket expense?**Advances your career**: Enhancing your skills with business or technical classes can provide a competitive differentiator. I completed business and technical courses that added to my credibility when I was a tech sales executive and a career consultant.
- **Improves job performance**: For those of you wanting a promotion to Director or VP, I strongly advise that you hone your presentation skills by joining a local

Toastmasters Club or signing up for a Dale Carnegie seminar. Early in my career, I completed a 2-month Carnegie course to gain confidence and up my communication delivery. There still was a gap in my verbal communication, but at least I narrowed it.

- **Leads to innovation**: It is as simple as doing personal research. I needed a new website and got five proposals. Nothing quite fit my needs, so I spent a month researching web design experts and tutorials to develop my customized site *www. resumetech.guru*.

## ADVANCED DEGREES & TECHNICAL CERTIFICATIONS

Another silver lining of Covid was that it provided a time for some of my clients to focus on their continued professional education. Several clients entered year-long MBA (Master of Business Administration) programs, a few completed AWS certifications within a month, and one joined a 6-month domain-specific university-sponsored program for AI (artificial intelligence).

### Executive MBA

While a traditional MBA typically supports early professionals seeking a management career, according to *U.S. News & World Report*, the average executive MBA student is 38 years old with 14 years of work experience.[4] The College Consensus *2021 Best Executive MBA Programs* composite ranking revealed the top 10 prestigious degrees:[5]

- University of Chicago - Booth School of Business
- University of Pennsylvania - The Wharton School
- Northwestern University - Kellogg School of Management
- MIT - Sloan School of Management
- Columbia University - Columbia Business School
- University of California - Berkeley Haas School of Business
- University of Virginia - Darden School of Business
- Yale University - School of Management
- Cornell University - SC Johnson College of Business
- Duke University - Fuqua School of Business

Do you wonder about the cost of attaining an Executive MBA at these prestigious B-schools? You will need to find $200,000, not exactly pocket change. Or your company might pay for it if you agree to work there for several more years. Typically, companies will have more senior positions available for that new and prestigious degree. If you are looking for a less expensive alternative in Seattle, I have you covered.

## UNIVERSITY OF WASHINGTON: 1-YEAR ACCELERATED MBA PROGRAM

As a U.S. military veteran, Christopher's service paid for a Bachelor of Science in Electrical Engineering degree from UCLA. His technical background included 10 years of operational leadership experience as a turnaround artist for startups, small businesses, and enterprise companies with Fortune 500 clients. Over the years, Christopher strengthened his strategic planning and business development skills for e-commerce, technology, training, and wireless verticals. After attaining VP and COO roles, he created his B2C (business-to-consumer) e-commerce startup for digital media. When Covid hit, it impacted his business, so he swiveled to pursue being hired as an employee in Seattle.

We collaborated on his career development plan targeting Fortune 500 companies. His top candidates were Prime Air (drone delivery service in development by Amazon) plus T-Mobile and Alaska Airlines. While Christopher developed his new implementation plan, the Seattle interview opportunities trickled in. Since companies and recruiters dealt with their work-at-home challenges during Covid, the majority did not place hiring as a critical initiative.

Fast forward to two months later, Christopher messaged me with the following note:

> "Happy to let you know I was accepted to an MBA program at the University of Washington, Foster School of Business starting June 22. It is an accelerated 1-year full-time program. I also found out the VA will help me pay for some of it. Big thanks for suggesting thinking of ways to enter programs that strengthen my resume and develop my skills! Hoping this will bridge a

gap while setting me up with solid
networking opportunities."

There have been several clients who have started or
completed this Seattle-based MBA program. Below
are the highlights for the 1-year University of Washington accelerated MBA program optimized for
global participants for your consideration.[6]

- **Term**: 1-year
- **Learning Process**: in-class lectures, case
  studies, interactive classroom experiences,
  executive speakers, and visits to area
  companies
- **Topics**: Global strategy, cross-cultural
  communications, finance, leadership,
  operations, and management
- **Student Profile**: Average age 37 years with
  12 years business experience with the top
  participant countries of origin Korea, Japan,
  and China
- **Tuition**: $90,000 full-term based on 2021
  rates
- **Requirements**: Bachelor's degree from a
  regionally accredited institution in the
  United States or an institution in Australia,
  the Bahamas, Canada, Ireland, New
  Zealand, Singapore, Trinidad and Tobago, or
  the United Kingdom. Documentation
  verifying that the applicant's undergraduate
  degree is from an institution where all
  instruction is in English. The candidate
  must take the GMAT and submit the score
  as part of the application process.

The other University of Washington degree offerings are a 2-year distance learning hybrid MBA for $78,000; 18-month technology management MBA for $87,400; 21-month executive MBA for $120,000; and 21-month full-time MBA for $105,000 non-resident or $71,200 resident year based on 2021 rates.

I checked on Christopher's progress, and during the MBA program, he interned at Microsoft for an Azure commercial marketplace project. Upon MBA graduation, he joined PwC in August 2021. It shows that an MBA can parlay into new career opportunities.

In Fall 2020, I met my client Arjun, a VP of software engineering at a €27 billion German-based multinational company. After 14 years at the same firm, he was ready for a career change. His professional goals were two-fold. First, he pursued taking on board member roles for startups and VC (venture capital) firms. Second, Arjun desired an IT domain senior executive function to elevate an organization to the next level of its growth. Arjun was an experimental person seeking his next leap into corporate leadership using his combined experience in IT and real estate investing.

Instead of landing his next VP role, Arjun attended The University of Texas at Austin's post-graduate program in Artificial Intelligence & Machine Learning: Business Applications. He expects to complete the 6-month program in 2021.

Arjun now serves as a technology and business growth advisory member for a California-based IT consulting firm (for his board member goal). Income is not a hurdle since he had a side-hustle of a family-owned million-dollar real estate investment company while working for his former company. He upped and quit working at the multinational company to pursue these courses of action.

## THE UNIVERSITY OF TEXAS AT AUSTIN POST-GRADUATE PROGRAM - ARTIFICIAL INTELLIGENCE (AI) & MACHINE LEARNING: BUSINESS APPLICATIONS

In this program you will earn a certificate from the #6 ranked university in business analytics to become an AI and machine learning expert.

- **Term**: 6 months
- **Learning Process**: Online recorded video format offers personalized interactive mentorship sessions, hands-on projects, and career development support. There is a 5- to 7-hour weekly time investment to complete the 11 modules and eight projects.
- **Tuition**: $3,500 based on 2021 rates

## AMAZON WEB SERVICES (AWS) CERTIFICATION

As an executive director of cloud architecture and customer engineering at a top cloud platform provider, my client Krithi had her eye on transitioning to high-growth Fortune 500 companies, recognized for their AI and cloud portfolios such as Amazon, Google, Microsoft, and Salesforce.

In late 2020, targeting an Amazon level 8 Senior Director role, she attained two AWS certifications:

Certified Cloud Practitioner (before interviewing) and Certified Solutions Architect Associate (after interviewing).

She landed a Solutions Architecture executive role at AWS four months from commencing her job search. How? It started by knowing a former colleague now employed at AWS, whom Krithi had impressed. She enhanced her branding by revamping her resume, LinkedIn profile, and hours of interviewing practice tailored towards Amazon's 14 leadership principles. Krithi finalized her decision between two job offers by connecting with another of my clients who knew both hiring managers.

Now happily employed at AWS, Krithi tackles large-scale digital transformation initiatives for multinationals, government, and Fortune 2000 clients as a passionate customer advocate. What impresses everyone is her advocacy for employee growth plus diversity and inclusion.

AWS recommends gaining 1-2 years of hands-on cloud computing experience before taking the certification exam. If you can set aside two months of intense study preparation, you are ready to take the test. The AWS Learning Library offers free access to video courses. The certification costs are relatively inexpensive, with the Cloud Practitioner exam at $100 while professional-level and specialty exams at $300 based on 2021 rates.

## COMBINATION CERTIFICATIONS: AWS, AZURE & GOOGLE

Gaspar is a 4-prong threat to his competition when seeking employment since—besides being one of my most intellectual clients coupled with a dry sense of humor—he has dozens of up-to-date certifications. Within the past five years, he attained the following items while serving in leadership roles as Accenture Managing Director, AWS Principal Architect, and Microsoft Senior Technology Director:

- AWS Cloud Practitioner
- Azure AI Fundamentals
- Azure Data Fundamentals
- Azure Power Platform Fundamentals
- Azure Solutions Architect Expert
- Google Cloud Certified – Associate Cloud Engineer
- MCSE Cloud Platform & Infrastructure

Executive recruiters flock to Gaspar because he is a true visionary, collaborator, and mentor with a platinum reputation within the industry.

As you can see, one-size does not fit all; there are different learning opportunities from a full-time pursuit or while you are working.

## EXERCISE: PUT IT INTO PRACTICE

Please go to your worksheet for **Roadmap #2: Investing in Yourself** and fill out the action plan.

**Action Plan**

1. Would it make sense to pursue an MBA?

   a) Yes or no?
   b) If yes, what are potential MBA programs
   in state or online?

2. Would it benefit my career to undertake a certification program?

   a) Yes or no?
   b) If yes, what are potential certifications for
   me to pursue?

## KEY TAKEAWAYS

The bottom line is that you need to determine the ROI (return on investment) for your career. Does it make sense to invest $3,500 for a technical certification or $200,000 for an executive MBA? The good news is that most employers will subsidize these costs. I got my MBA right after completing my BBA from The University of Texas at Austin. I can say that the MBA enhanced my career opportunities. On the other hand, I have clients without college degrees that have stellar careers.

In this chapter for **Investing in Yourself**, you learned about:

- different learning styles,
- benefits of continuous adult education, and
- potential advanced degrees and technical certifications.

The question is, after everything I have told you, are you ready to hit the books? It is one thing to have continuing education on your to-do list; it is another to set aside time for you to do it.

In the next chapter, we will chat about the merits of joining a board of directors.

# BOARDS OF DIRECTORS & PROFESSIONAL ASSOCIATIONS

Staring at the retirement countdown clock, Elizabeth reached out to me. She was excited at the prospect of retiring in 13 months as a senior director in AI and Enterprise Software, although she had additional career aspirations.

When I asked Elizabeth why after 20 years at her current company she needed my help, her response was, "I am considering my options after retirement for consulting roles or at a non-profit."

I asked why a non-profit, and she said, "My ideal next step is contributing to a larger vision, leading change, solving complex problems while working from home—maybe going to the office once a week. My focus is giving back, sharing knowledge, and empowering others."

So began our journey to position Elizabeth to either join a non-profit board or lead one. Besides nonprofits, corporations and startups recruit my clients for board positions; they receive annual stipends or equity positions. Or the opposite, they actually pay to sit on a board.

I am amazed at how many of my colleagues do not focus outside of their corporate bubble. They can spend 15 years of their career without ever joining an outside board or professional association. With my clients, it is a different story since we discuss their next steps, and I bring up the subject.

In this chapter about **Boards of Directors & Professional Associations**, I will review how to:

- join boards for thought leadership,
- consider not-for-profits for making a social impact, and
- belong to a professional organization for networking opportunities.

When I checked LinkedIn in August 2021, over six million individuals featured "board member" on their profiles. Exploring this further on a personal front, 25% of my LinkedIn connections are board members. If you are interested in joining a board, this next section is for you. If not, please skip ahead in the chapter to determine if belonging to a professional association is in your future. I will give you a hint; it should be.

## JOINING A BOARD OF DIRECTORS

I uncovered through online research and reaching out to my network that there are primarily two types of boards to join: corporate for-profit and not-for-profit. There is a different rationale for joining either type.

Before we go into detail, let us start with the process of joining a board. It is all about who you know and who knows about you. Most board of directors placements come through their network visibility; board recruiting agencies arrange most Fortune 2000 corporate positions. Your experience, integrity, and personal brand image established at speaking engagements, conferences, networking events, and your online presence factor into a potential fit for a board.

According to professional and organizational development consultant Carter McNamara: "A board of directors is a group of people legally charged with the responsibility to govern a corporation. In a for-profit corporation, the board of directors is responsible to the stockholders. In a non-profit corporation, the board reports to stakeholders, particularly the local communities which the non-profit serves."[1]

There is no set membership number, selection criteria, term limit, or meeting schedule. Corporate boards have members, usually called directors, whom the stockholders elect. In a privately held company, the owner's founders select members without a formal election.

There is a chairperson or president, vice-chair or vice-president, secretary, and treasurer from an organizational perspective. In my research, I encountered anywhere from 3 to 31 members appearing on boards. The number of members may impact reaching consensus on issues, so typically there is an uneven number of individuals for voting tiebreakers. There are set terms for membership sometimes, which can either be voted on or simply assigned. Understandably, there is more rigor tied to for-profit corporate boards due to state and federal regulations. You, being on a board has legal implications.

If you wonder about the gender breakdown, it is mostly a men's club. Within the Russell 3000 Index, women hold only 24.4% of total board seats, according to the March 2021 research conducted by the national non-profit 50/50 Women on Boards™.[2]

## BOARD MEMBERS' SPECIFIC RESPONSIBILITIES

Corporate and not-for-profit boards should have responsibilities outlined in their annual proxy statement, constitution, bylaws, or declaration. If not, reconsider joining, since your obligations are unclear. BoardSource provides the following 10 guidelines for responsibilities.[3]

- Determine the organization's mission and purpose
- Select an executive
- Support the executive and review his or her performance
- Ensure effective organizational planning
- Ensure adequate resources
- Manage resources effectively
- Determine and monitor the organization's products, services, and programs

- Enhance organization's public image
- Serve as a court of appeal
- Assess its own performance

As I mentioned previously, I am a Walmart stockholder and located their 8-page corporate governance guidelines on their website. It details director qualifications, board responsibilities, committees, director access to officers, associates, and outside advisors, director compensation, director orientation and continuing education, CEO evaluation and management succession, and annual performance evaluation. Below are the highlights:

- The majority of the directors should meet the NYSE American Company Guide Rule 802 requiring that a majority of the board of directors of a listed company be independent. An independent director is not an executive officer or employee of the company.
- Nominees for director will be selected based on outstanding achievement in their personal careers; broad experience; expertise in matters of particular relevance to the Company; wisdom; integrity; ability to make independent, analytical inquiries; understanding of the business environment; and willingness to devote adequate time to board duties.
- A majority vote shall elect each director in an uncontested election.
- Within five years of joining the board, each new outside director is required to own an

amount of shares, restricted stock, or stock units equal in value to five times the annual cash retainer offered to each director at the time the director joined the board.

- The number of directors that shall constitute the board shall not be less than 3 nor more than 20.
- An outside director is expected to serve for at least 6 years.
- The board will meet at least 4 times per year.

## COMPENSATION & TIME ALLOCATION

A *CEOWorld* article explained that "total compensation for a board seat will vary depending on company size, public or private, the number of meetings and the responsibilities involved. This compensation is generally in the form of cash retainers, equity grants, and meeting fees."[4] If board members are not locally based, companies compensate them for travel expenses related to meetings and retreats. For-profit board members typically receive compensation, while not-for-profit do not.

On the Harvard Law School Forum for Corporate Governance & Financial Regulation, Diane Lerner posted: "Director pay levels tend to be very closely clustered together, unlike the wider distribution of executive pay. For example, the 25th percentile of total compensation for the S&P 500 sample is $230,000, and the 75th percentile is $295,000 compared to a median of $260,000. This means the vast majority of S&P 500 companies pay Directors within $35,000 of the median."[5]

What makes headlines are the large payouts, including 21st Century Fox's average compensation per board member of $2.58MM (million) and Regeneron Pharmaceuticals Inc. at $2.17MM per board member. According to PayScale's database, $60,000 is the average salary for a member of a board of directors with a $9,000 bonus and $12,500 for profit sharing. For being a chairman, PayScale notes, the average salary is more than double at $146,810.

Depending on the board type, the time commitment varies. Not-for-profits tend toward a monthly meeting cadence with a 2-hour allotment along with ad hoc time for being a part of a project committee. Several boards with worthy causes reached out for me to join, but I declined because of the time commitment. Sometimes it is not the perfect fit.

For-profit boards vary from quarterly all-day meetings to just a phone call relationship in an advisory board position. One executive I spoke with noted there was one annual meeting for its members to sit down with the CEO, to discuss business strategy and quiz the CEO on funding, tech, and sales.

There are many benefits to being on a board.

- **Personal Branding**: You can raise your leadership profile by your association for a cause or company you support; highlight your passion through your online feed, executive bio, and resume.

As acknowledged by a CIO client: "For a pure not-for-profit, there is no residual financial return. It is my time to be philanthropic, plus it looks good on my CV. Per the board, they encourage you to advertise your involvement." It is a win-win for both parties.

> **Knowledge**: Learning about how others
> think can expand your perspective.

A current board president commented: "I am amazed at the wide variety of opinions. We would bring in an industry expert, and five members' take-aways would be unique."

That knowledge works two ways. After a lengthy vetting process, one executive accepted an invitation to join the board. The hesitation was by the company since sometimes a board is uncertain about what it needs until it sees it.

- **Networking**: Choose the proper board; you make contacts for life similar to joining a college fraternity or sorority. I encourage my clients to volunteer or join committees now to network for other career adventures or have an exit strategy upon retirement.

A board treasurer shared: "When I was serving on the finance committee, I had no idea I would establish a strong bond with other members. I would not have met these people in my industry. It is the common mission that made us tight-knit."

- **Community Involvement**: Every Fortune 500 company I worked for has sponsored employee volunteer activities to benefit the community. My former sales client base included not-for-profits such as Bloodworks Northwest, Seattle Children's Hospital, and World Vision. CenturyLink supported all three with gifts-in-kind, monetary donations, and a volunteer workforce.

I polled my connections, and each one would continue to be on a board or join a new one. There are triumphs to be celebrated for being on a board, where you can make a difference plus feel great. Please note that it is not all joy and happiness participating on a board, as one of my acquaintances was surprised by the amount of aggression for participating on a not-for-profit board.

Whether it is for giving back or helping drive a company's mission, joining a board of directors can provide fulfillment outside of your everyday work life. If you are not quite ready to join a board, it is time to evaluate belonging to a professional association.

## PROFESSIONAL ASSOCIATIONS

Based on the latest IRS statistics, there are close to 300,000 not-for-profit charitable organizations, with professional associations being a subset.[6] Do you belong to one? If not, join one to augment your career path.

In my coaching practice, I review hundreds of resumes and LinkedIn profiles. My sample size reveals that only 15% of clients belong to a professional association. I believed the percentage would be in the 50% range, so this was quite a revelation.

Marketing General Incorporated's *2018 Membership Marketing Benchmarking Report* survey of 821 professional associations revealed that membership numbers are experiencing year-over-year growth.[7] As for why members joined, the association's leadership disclosed that 58% of their members joined to network with others in their field, and 26% signed up to learn best practices.

Since my focus is technology executives, the most predominant association I see on resumes is the IEEE, which claims it is the world's largest technical professional organization.[8] My clients who belong are part of the 400,000 members participating in over 160 countries. A few clients take part in the IEEE technical communities developing standards or speaking at one of the 1,800 annual conferences and events.

As described under the U.S. Internal Revenue Code Section 501(c)3, the IEEE qualifies as a tax-exempt organization, which means it is eligible to receive charitable contributions. If you join the IEEE, your membership dues are tax-deductible. Membership pricing varies by geography, professional or student status, and your industry. In 2021 if you join as a professional, the IEEE dues range from $205 to $208, depending on your region. When my husband joined IEEE early in his career, GE and Corning Glass paid for his membership dues. Check with your company to see if the same applies for you.

This year I joined the WomenTech Network as a community member and mentor. The association's mission is to inspire one million women, minorities, and their allies in science and engineering. I signed up to give back and keep up to date on technology trends. When I was a marketing professional at Sprint, I joined the American Marketing Association and attended local meetings in Kansas City. It was a monthly opportunity to network with those both inside and outside my company. During our luncheons a keynote speaker discussed industry hot topics, providing a learning aspect. The membership directory and sponsored events helped vet some of my future employees.

I see the benefits of joining a professional association for career transitions. Zhang, who I mentored, wanted to focus on cybersecurity. He joined an association and became a Seattle chapter president. This action supported his job search efforts for moving from being an IT manager at a small-sized business, to joining AWS in July 2021 as a security engineer.

Now it is time for you to act on escaping the confines of your corporate environment and pursue a board position or join a professional association.

## RCISE: PUT IT INTO PRACTICE

ease go to your worksheet for **Roadmap #2: Board of Directors & Professional Associations** and fill out the action plan.

**Action Plan**

1. Board Membership. List 3 not-for-profits and contact them about joining
2. Professional Association: Check out the following for consideration to join

   a) https://www.ieee.org/
   b) http://www.cloudcomputingassn.org

## KEY TAKEAWAYS

Joining a corporate board provides powerful connections, although legal and financial considerations weigh in the balance. A seat on a not-for-profit board is more attainable than a corporate board and has the added benefit of supporting a worthy cause, but there is a higher time investment. I strongly encourage you to join a professional association for the networking opportunities and knowledge base.

Congratulations on completing the second career roadmap point for **C-Suite Advice**! You have learned about best practices and client observations for:

- thinking like a CEO,
- benefiting from mentor and coach collaborations,

- investing in your continuing education, and
- joining boards and professional associations for networking opportunities and social impact.

In the next section of the book, I will discuss how to assess and develop your personal brand to become a recruiter magnet.

Felix ?

## Career Roadmap Point #3
# Personal Brand

For this third roadmap point, it is time to define your **Personal Brand** for your next role. When you are not in the room, what does your team or boss say about you? That, my friend, describes your personal brand. It doubles as the key to your superpower for career moves within the tech industry.

People arrive at my virtual office trying to figure out their brand positioning for their next role. That was the case with Raj, the engineering manager at AWS that I previously talked about. Although he had been on the other side of the job search equation recruiting and interviewing his staff of 60 people, he was challenged on the best way to present himself for the next executive role. Furthermore, Raj felt at a deficit for not understanding the best practices of a U.S. job search. Although he had a 10-year tenure at AWS, he moved here nine years ago from his native India, so he did not know how to navigate a search in the U.S.

Raj's LinkedIn profile was impressive having worked at four distinct billion-dollar companies across vertical markets in consulting, manufacturing, and e-commerce. Based upon a solid academic foundation with a Master's in Computer Science, he had attained LinkedIn skills endorsements for product management, software development, and agile methodology. In order for Raj to become an online executive recruiter magnet, I suggested five optimization opportunities in his headline, career summary, job descriptions, leadership skill endorsements, and virtual recommendations.

During our initial consult call, I asked, "Why are you interested in leaving Amazon after a decade, and how can I help you?"

He responded, "10 years is too long to stay here because I will be branded as an Amazonian. I am finally free from the U.S. working visa restrictions. I currently manage 60 people, including engineering managers, principal engineers, and principal program managers. For geography, I am not limiting myself to Seattle; it could be Austin or Southern California but definitely not the Bay area."

I probed for further detail, and he shared, "I'm looking to have a personal brand message that comes through in my resume and LinkedIn profile. How do I effectively brand myself, so my resume stands out to companies? I have not done it for a long time. Since I have been in middle management at Amazon, my goal is to step up to the director level."

Raj concisely outlined his goals in seeking a career consultant. He wanted to focus within the tech domain for an executive role and be at the forefront of human-assisted AI and virtual reality to drive a 10x scale at a FinTech like Robinhood or Fidelity Investments. He needed to create a resume to start his job search and polish his LinkedIn profile to increase online recruiter visibility and discovery. And so, we framed Raj's personal brand.

At this third roadmap point for your **Personal Brand**, I will discuss how to:

- harness your superpower,
- identify your top skills,
- create an elevator pitch,
- embrace social media, and
- address diversity and inclusion.

# WHAT ARE YOUR SUPERPOWERS?

A post appeared on LinkedIn voicing an opinion about the flawed concept of a personal brand. The poster was quite indignant, pointing out that we are humans versus products. More power to her for having this perspective, but the financial reality is billion-dollar ecosystems exist related to personal branding.

My perspective is proceeding with what works best for you. For me, I'm all in on personal brand for your career since I benefited from it. Oh, and it is what I do for a living.

Your superpowers are qualities that drive your career success and make you stand out from other executive search candidates. Employers sometimes ask the superpower question to learn about your unique strengths for the hiring position. The superpower does not need to be X-ray vision, rather it is being a puzzle-solver, agent of change, technical visionary, or trusted advisor. Your superpowers form the foundation of your personal brand; highlight these on your resume, LinkedIn professional profile, and in job interviews.

In this chapter, you will uncover your **Superpowers** by:

- understanding the importance of personal branding,
- establishing your point of view,
- learning tips on developing your brand, and
- promoting yourself to become a recruiter magnet.

What exactly is a personal brand for your career? Let's start with the familiar notion of a brand.

## DEFINITION OF A PRODUCT BRAND

How many of you have heard of Chanel? For most women, the Chanel logo is synonymous with clothes, fragrances, handbags, and watches. According to *Forbes Magazine,* Chanel has a $12.8B brand value and ranks #52 on the 2020 annual list that identifies "The World's Most Valuable Brands."[1] Apple ranked #1 with a $241.2B brand value on the same list, which increased 17% year-over-year. Ironically, you can wear both on your wrist, but for pricing, Chanel will cost you more than an Apple Watch; beauty over function at a price.

Interbrand, a subsidiary of advertising conglomerate Omnicom, evaluates global brands based on a range of factors, including how well a brand is known, how well it is regarded, and how much it contributes to the parent company's financial success. In their "Best Global Brands 2020 Rankings," Apple landed the #1 spot followed by Amazon, Microsoft, Google, Samsung, Coca-Cola, Toyota, Mercedes-Benz, McDonald's, and Disney.[2]

Think of the Starbucks mermaid, the McDonald's golden arches, and the Amazon smile from A to Z, which you see online, at retail storefronts, within emails, and on packaging. For me, these brands evoke sentiments of quality, confidence, enjoyment, good value, and likeability.

Now your personal brand: Do you evoke a positive +ve or negative vibe? It depends on the audience; we don't have 100% ardent fans. My advice is to surround yourself with supporters and reach out to companies in your job search with missions and values you admire. After all, you will hang out there physically and mentally for over 60 hours weekly.

## POINT OF VIEW (POV)

Let us get back to eavesdropping on what colleagues say about you when you leave a virtual conference room.

When people encounter you within the business environment, whether in person, phone calls, emails, blogs, or LinkedIn, how would they describe you? Every day we position ourselves for work or personal needs. Within the professional environment, encounters with colleagues, clients, or management include communicating your ideas to gain mindshare or sway opinions. The net result ranges from developing relationships, winning business, garnering job promotions, or keeping your job.

Whenever I work with a new client, I ask them why they selected me. It is an excellent way to obtain branding feedback. Clients most appreciate that I customize a proposal to their needs after evaluating their request and LinkedIn profile. Some women relate to my gender. Other clients want my tech career management experience to advise them on their next career adventure.

During our discussions I ask them to provide five adjectives that others would use to describe them. It is an intriguing question with various responses and helps me position their brand online and within their resume. Responses typically are positive, such as "responsible" and "trustworthy," although a client jotted down a negative attribute related to their Emotional Intelligence (EQ) as "cold;" perhaps the reason for no promotion?

> "In countless studies, all over the world, emotional intelligence has been strongly linked to both personal and professional success."[3]

I believe a lack of EQ hinders one's advancement. The good news is you can overcome it with work and guidance. Knowing your handicaps is the first step to improvement.

LinkedIn provides a solid method for identifying your skills; in the "skills & endorsement" section of your profile, the top 3 skills appear ranked by your professional network's endorsements. These a related to your industry knowledge and interpersonal skills. You can reinforce specific skills by asking colleagues for endorsements. Since LinkedIn is Applicant Tracking System (ATS) searchable, recruiters search within your skills section and About summary to match executive role job requirements.

## PERSONAL BRANDING TIPS

Help is on hand for developing your personal brand. See what members of the Forbes Agency Council share about creating a solid personal brand:[4]

- Embrace authenticity
- Give to receive
- Start yesterday
- Focus on your superpower
- Develop a distribution on LinkedIn
- Showcase your personality
- Try video
- Remain consistent
- Understand your values
- Determine what you are interested in

My favorite tip is to focus on your superpower. Do you know what yours is? If not, it is time check your LinkedIn profile for skill endorsements and recommendations. Go ahead and poll your friends mentors.

A colleague believes my business superpowers are research and analysis, a common bond for us. As you are aware, I am a fan of an Excel spreadsheet and seeking information.

Another favorite tip from the above Forbes list is determining your interest, which for me has evolved. After an early retirement, I volunteered as a career consultant at Dress for Success, which prompted friends to ask if I could help them. Better yet, they will pay for my expertise in uncovering their next career opportunity, developing an elevator pitch, creating a resume, writing cover letters, and over-hauling their LinkedIn profile. Bingo! A consulting practice was born within six months of business case development based upon competitive analysis, industry research, expert feedback, networking, pricing strategy, seminar presentations, and trial runs.

Three years later, I thoroughly enjoy collaborating with my clients and cheer their wins.

## PROJECTING YOURSELF

In the career environment, your personal brand helps you land your next role. Thinking about how others see you, I recommend paying attention to the details that project your brand. These vary and may change on your career path. The focus points below are for those seeking Fortune company management positions:

- **LinkedIn**: When was the last time you updated your profile? Suppose that you are looking for a management job. In that case, 80% of recruiters look at your profile, whether you applied via an executive recruiter, LinkedIn, CareerBuilder, Indeed, ExecThread, or the corporate website. Do you show a photo of a smiling professional? Yes, you can use an Android or iPhone camera shot; please make sure it has you in a professional pose, without your friend's shoulder or family pet—those photos are great for Instagram or Facebook! By posting content and creating articles on LinkedIn, you reinforce to your network your expertise and interests. My cadence for creating executive career advice articles is 2X per month, while posts average several per week.

- **Phone Etiquette**: If someone calls you, how do you answer the phone or what is your voicemail message? I follow the lead of my executive mentor with, "Hello, this is Monique Montanino." It portrays confidence versus the curt "Hello." The same applies to joining a corporate conference call.

- **Personal Website**: If you have a website related to business; fabulous. Suppose you have a website pertaining to a personal hobby; fantastic. Make sure your personal beliefs are not offensive to a potential employer's values or mission. If you think that is ridiculous, it is not. It has diminished the promotions of several of my colleagues. It is a balancing act for their right to free speech. At Fortune companies, they conduct media training for what and how you can communicate about the company. Project that same effort toward your brand.

- **Social Media**: How did the world exist before Facebook, Instagram, and Twitter? Actually, quite nicely. I did not have active accounts until several years ago. My career advice targets my client base in tech and IT seeking an executive promotion, specifically, keep your social media accounts focused on your professional persona without personal views and lightening rod topics of politics or religion. What you believe is your right to communicate might be at odds with an employer. Once again, from a job search perspective, I recommend keeping your thoughts to yourself and your friends. On the flip side, some of my coaching colleagues use their very vocal approach to attract their clients; it is their niche. I applaud them for their strategy and results.

- **Correspondence**: Corporations provide auto signature email blocks for their employees to use, including name, title, address, phone, email, and logo. Create one for your personal email accounts and cover letters when corresponding with recruiters, hiring managers, and professional colleagues. It not only looks more polished, but it also provides accessible contact information. When was the last time someone sent you an email, received a request to call or text, and you had to search for their phone number? Remove that burden for recruiters to contact you.

- **Resume**: If you have not written a resume in a couple of years, take the time to google best resume advice or hire an expert. If you are applying online, an ATS will not appreciate: color, photos, inserted graphic lines, columns, or items in the footer or header. By contrast, ATS embraces 1,000 words, white space, standard margins, professional summary, personal brand keywords list, and job description with bulleted accomplishment metrics that provide your potential employer with reasons to hire you. You can check how your resume will score for an ATS job posting by using a free tool at *www.jobscan.co*.

## EXERCISE: PUT IT INTO PRACTICE

Please go to the worksheet for **Roadmap #3: What Are Your Superpowers?** and fill out the action plan. You're getting back to my initial question about what people think of you when you are not in the room. If you're not eavesdropping, how can you find out? It is easy; just ask them.

### Action Plan

1. Write down for your personal brand your top 3 leadership skills. Either refer to your LinkedIn profile or reach out to colleagues. Determine which skills are your superpowers.
2. Describe your top 3 domain skills that you need to reinforce to attract recruiters to

your resume, LinkedIn, and discuss in your interviewing sessions.

## KEY TAKEAWAYS

We all have a professional brand; by determining your superpowers, you will stand out from the competition. I asked my client Irina to describe mine. She responded by text message: "Go-getter relationship builder. You are clear, concise, and get to the point. Type A and you wear it proudly." By the way, that describes Irina too.

In this chapter for **Superpowers**, you learned about:

- understanding the importance of personal branding,
- establishing your point of view,
- learning tips on developing your brand, and
- promoting yourself to become a recruiter magnet.

In the next chapter, we will be heading to the elevator. Ready to push some buttons?

## ELEVATOR PITCH

Do you cringe at the thought of introducing yourself in a group setting? Does responding to "so tell me about yourself" in a job interview send shivers up your spine? Never fear; we tackle this subject now.

The irony is I am 100% confident speaking during initial consulting sessions whereby clients are trying to figure out if I am their person. Speaking as the lone presenter on webinars with 100 attendees, no problem. It is the group thing that makes me nervous. It brings me no joy to introduce myself in a cohort session, which I had to do a dozen times in the past year.

My junior high school days in—wait for it—a drama class created my brain chaos. A poem I wrote called "The Lonely Child" earned me the opportunity to participate in a district-wide reading competition; this event was a new situation. More dubiously, I cannot recall practicing for the recital, but I remember freaking out and not being able to read out loud the day of the competition. Keep in mind, I wrote the poem, but, no matter, I literally froze after the first line of the poem, zero words emitted from my mouth, leaving a 12-year-old crestfallen and marked for life.

No big deal, right? Since just junior high? Nope, I replay that bad old tape in my brain every time I have to introduce myself in a group setting. There is a light at the end of the tunnel for me and you if you have the same issue.

In this chapter, we will focus on your **Elevator Pitch** by:

- defining the components.
- creating one for job interviews, and
- gaining confidence in your delivery.

One of the first things I ask my clients as a career advocate is: "Tell me about yourself."

It appears like an innocuous question, but it is usually met with hesitation. The reason I ask this is to determine if and how I can assist my client to have a successful journey. Is this for an internal company move? Promotion at the next company? Transition to a new industry? Or employment after a layoff?

After we identify the focus, we can craft an up-to-date personal brand image strategy. Believe it or not, 90% of the time, it takes a 60-minute discussion to synthesize a concise answer for the "tell me about yourself" question. I call this your elevator pitch.

A VP of Business Strategy told me the following when I asked him to describe himself in three concise sentences:

> "I developed a deep level of expertise on the E2E business SaaS model—understood business processes, technology solutions, key business metrics, organizational impacts, and customer journey implications from marketing, through sales, contracting, fulfillment, provisioning, deployment, services, support, and ongoing customer success."

Would you consider this an Emmy-worthy performance if you were an executive recruiter? How about this one for a Demand Generation Director?

> "I am a farmer. Not in the traditional sense of growing crops from seeds, rather planting a marketing digital construct to boost the sales leads funnel for customer acquisition."

> "About those marketing seeds... They germinated in high school with the DECA (Distributive Education Clubs of America) initiative. The program prepares emerging leaders and entrepreneurs in high schools and colleges around the globe. It unleashed a massive entrepreneurial hunger."

> "My expertise is driving revenue for early-stage startups and SMBs."

> "Across the past four years, I collaborated

with five startups from Series A through D with over $300MM in VC funding. The results? After deploying custom GTM strategies and scaling marketing engines, around $50MM appeared within their sales funnels."

"When it comes to demand generation, leading smaller teams who release high-octane SEM programs and run fast is my nirvana."

I gave a standing ovation for candidate #2 because it made me lean in. Who knew there were farmers in tech that drove results? **Tell a story and people will listen**.

## DEFINING THE COMPONENTS

Philip Crosby, a technician and author who contributed to quality management practices, suggested "individuals should have a pre-prepared speech that can deliver information regarding themselves or a quality that they can provide within a short period of time, namely the amount of time of an elevator ride for if an individual finds themselves on an elevator with a prominent figure. Essentially, an elevator pitch allows an individual to pitch themselves or an idea to a person who is high up in a company, with very limited time."[1]

My formal training on elevator pitch creation happened a decade ago at a Miller Heiman Strategic Selling course when I was a CenturyLink sales executive. Miller Heiman is well-versed in solution selling training, which ultimately is what you need to position yourself for your next career opportunity. You are positioning yourself to meet the corporations' needs with your unique skills and background. Each of my Miller Heiman classmates had to create and deliver their elevator pitch to the class. We practiced 1:1 with another classmate before the epic room revelation. Of course, I had high anxiety the night before returning to my junior high school brain freeze, but I felt I nailed it on the actual day. Truth be told, the instructor and colleagues mentioned, "nice job."

Creating an elevator pitch is challenging, since it is not a routine task to talk about yourself as a personal commercial within a 30-second timeframe. Well, unless you are a consultant like me. Initially, it feels very uncomfortable, but once you master it, it is absolutely empowering. I recite mine on every initial and closing consulting call. I just did it today; twice!

> "I have arrived full circle from corporate brand consulting at Coca-Cola, General Motors, and the U.S. Army to personal brand consulting for technology executives. After 18 years as a marketing and sales executive at Fortune 500 companies, I retired early four years ago. I got bored, became a volunteer career advocate, and my former colleagues mentioned they would pay me for help on their resumes and LinkedIn profiles. My personal brand consulting practice for technology executives was born."

This pitch, coupled with an overview of my services and process, closes the deal for client engagements.

An elevator pitch succinctly defines who you are within the business environment. After my client develops their elevator pitch, we weave components of it into their resume and LinkedIn profile; this is essential for networking events and job interviews. The first question a recruiter or hiring manager will ask you is to summarize who you are. This astute preparation enables you to respond without a rambling answer.

In summary, an elevator pitch is a short description of your personal brand, explaining who you are, what you have done, and why you are the perfect person for the job. This is your opportunity to communicate your brand to any listener within a short time period. Add enthusiasm and personality so recruiters will lean in; you will thank me later.

## CREATING A PITCH FOR JOB INTERVIEWS

Remember, within the career environment, the idea of an elevator pitch is providing a compelling peek about yourself, so the other person wants to know more. It is about engagement and connection. Think of it as a speed dating introduction within the business context. From a resume and LinkedIn profile perspective, it starts with your headline. What title best describes you? Next, let's layer three components that succinctly summarize you:

- explain who you are from a career perspective,

- place your experience into context, and
- highlight intangible strengths you deliver to a hiring company.

Here are some samples, feel free to clone and own, for your pitch.

- Headline: Chief Information Security Officer (CISO) | Cyber Security Thought Leader | Speaker

"For 19 years, I have been spearheading the organizational understanding of the ever-changing threat landscape. I work with cross-disciplinary research teams at AWS, mapping data, and intelligence into actionable insights. I am an award-winning speaker, author, blogger, and mentor at the Cyber Security & Cloud Expo and Gartner Security & Risk Management Summits. I am continuously wearing a white hat."

- Headline: DevOps Engineering Director

"Let us just say I am an unconventional thinker. My experience is grounded within Linux and Unix Administration. For over 15 years, I have been designing, implementing, and managing cutting-edge deployment automation of cloud resources. I am proud of being an acclaimed troubleshooter in dev, test, and production environments. I am excited about building the future at the confluence of agile, data, and cloud computing."

- Headline: VP Engineering | Software Product Lifecycle Executive | ITIL & PMP Certified

"I have more than 15 years of IT management experience at two Fortune 200 companies, Microsoft and AWS. As a result, I am a recognized leader in technology product management. I am fortunate to have a team builder mentality delivering technical project requirements on time; in turn, my direct reports tend to follow me when I join different companies."

- Headline: Chief Marketing Officer (CMO) | Fortune 500 | Technology Hardware

"I am an evangelical business marketer, and product strategist transforming the way corporations attract B2B and B2C clients. I offer 25 years of CMO experience at Fortune 500 and IT startups, bringing a thoughtful perspective and branding savvy. I am entrepreneurial at heart and a Forbes speaker recognized for my impassioned approach and colorful ideas."

## GAINING CONFIDENCE IN DELIVERY

I took a Dale Carnegie speaking course. Went to a speech therapist. Read umpteen books on public speaking. Observed the best speakers. My biggest revelation is listening to comedians unraveling punch-lines. They know storytelling and command a laugh starting with a premise, a personal experience, and a summary thought. It flows throughout their comedy set, and I admire the stand-up comedian George Carlin for his brain droppings. Yes, he published a book with that title, which speaks to me in many ways.

It all boils down to structure and practice. If there is one takeaway I have learned about being a successful technology executive, it is developing and delivering a great story. Storytellers win.

In 2021 there were several opportunities to create an elevator pitch for myself for different projects. A homework assignment in my writing class was to create a 20-second book spiel for *Clicks, Tricks, & Golden Handcuffs*. You know, the book you bought and are reading? Then our instructor, Dr. Cindy, The Expert's Ghostwriter, sponsored an author debut salon session. The junior high school flashbacks zipped through my mind, so I got busy.

For my 5-minute book debut, I read Dr. Cindy's writing class notes, replayed former author debuts, and watched dozens of U-Tube videos about book readings.

Since it was winter I had migrated from Seattle to Austin, so my daily 3-mile walk was around Lady Bird Lake. It is where I practiced delivering my 5-minute speech out loud, looking ahead, and not caring if anyone thought I was a mental case. When I got home over dinner, my husband heard my speech.

After two weeks straight hearing my pitch, Pat threw up his hands and said, "Stop, I can't take it anymore."

I continued to carry on and then grilled him, "How did I do? Do I still pause? Any words sound off? What are your thoughts on using my hands like an Italian?"

All the effort paid off in two ways. First, when I watched the replay of my 5-minute book debut, I smiled since it went off without a hitch, with even Dr. Cindy saying I did not look nervous. I was calm, yet excited. Second, Pat now understands what I do for a living—instead of saying I am a resume writer, he can eloquently state that I am a career consultant for technology executives.

## EXERCISE: PUT IT INTO PRACTICE

Please go to your worksheet for **Roadmap #3: Elevator Pitch** and fill out the action plan. Knock it out of the park with your superpowers!

### Action Plan

It is time to create your elevator pitch. Limit it to 3-5 sentences and time it using a video or phone app. Practice makes perfect.

1. Who are you from a career perspective?
2. Place your experience in context.
3. What intangible strengths do you bring to the hiring company?

## KEY TAKEAWAYS

I am the poster child for coming from a junior high school brain freeze to an uber-confident elevator pitchwoman. Okay, maybe uber is a bit much. Be sure that you know the components and understand it takes practice; I am confident you too can hit it out of the park.

In this chapter, about your **Elevator Pitch**, you learned about:

- the components for one,
- creating one for job interviews, and
- how to gain confidence in your delivery.

Are you a social butterfly? If not, we will unpack the importance of being one or acting like one in the next chapter.

# SOCIAL MEDIA PRESENCE

Did you know that 82% of the U.S. population has a social networking profile?[1] Since this statistic probably includes you, it is imperative to manage your social media presence for business dating; i.e., interviewing for a job or attracting a recruiter.

How you appear online contributes to your career professional brand, whether that is your business profile on LinkedIn or your personal Facebook account.

In a Harris Poll of 1,005 U.S. hiring decision-makers, "70% believe employers should screen all applicants' social media profiles, while the majority (67%) say they use social networking sites to research potential job candidates."[2] Also, 21% would pass on a job seeker if they lacked a social media account.

If a hiring manager googled you, how would you show up? Would you be in the consideration set if a recruiter searched LinkedIn to fill an executive-level position at a cloud enterprise company or a startup? If you don't know, it's time to take control of your electronic footprint for your next career opportunity.

In this chapter, you will focus on your **Social Media Presence** by:

- auditing your virtual presence,
- reviewing top professional branding outlets, and
- accessing your LinkedIn Social Selling Index score.

## SOCIAL MEDIA STATISTICS

A Statista report published in February 2021 revealed Facebook (rebranded Meta) was the first social network to surpass one billion registered accounts. The company currently owns the top four social media platforms, each one having over one billion monthly active users: Facebook, WhatsApp, Facebook Messenger, and Instagram.[3] The report discusses other social network platforms; some were not on my radar. This list appears below rank-ordered by active users from 2.74 billion on Facebook down to 300 million on Quora. LinkedIn did not make the graph due to lower active monthly users, measuring 240 million.

- Facebook
- YouTube
- WhatsApp
- Facebook Messenger

- Instagram
- Wexin/WeChat
- TikTok
- QQ
- Douyin
- Sina Weibo
- Telegram
- Snapchat
- Kuaishou
- Pinterest
- Reddit
- Twitter
- Quora

Getting back to my initial question, how do you appear on these social media sites to a hiring manager? Are your accounts locked down or wide-open? If the latter, I strongly advise that you keep a prospective company in mind regarding to your postings and images. Are you entitled to your personal opinions outside the company about politics, religion, hobbies, and newsmakers? Absolutely. I am not saying to squash your thoughts; keep in mind another person's potential conflicting point of view. In short, do not say anything negative on social media; it might hurt you eventually.

## LESSONS FROM GOOGLE

Yes, I do google myself, not out of vanity, rather for optimizing my business opportunities. My first and last name results lean toward a professional POV with LinkedIn, Instagram, and my website *www.re-sumetech.guru* securing the top three spots followed by *theorg.com*, Twitter handle @resumetechguru, and my Google Business listing *resumetech-guru.business.site*. There is logic to the top three since I update them routinely. As a modest user of The Org and Twitter, those are head-scratchers.

For my consulting brand presence, I conduct a quarterly Google search. I pay attention to how I fare based on keywords clients would use to find me, including "Seattle tech resume writer" and "executive career coach." Initially, I spent a large amount of time on my two Google business listings, geo-targeting Seattle and Austin. It took a couple of years for my business name, Resume Tech Guru, to appear on the first page of a Google search based upon the keywords of "Seattle resume writer."

When I launched my website a couple of years ago, I paid for Google AdWords and ran several advertising campaigns. Although they did not yield the referral results I hoped for, the analytics showed what keywords drove traffic to my websites. Good news: resume writing was a top keyword. Bad news: resume builder was also a top keyword, but I do not offer an automated version. In the first year of my consulting practice, a Monster Insights report revealed that my website bounce rate was high. If you are not familiar with the term, it is the percentage of website visitors who navigate away (or bounce off your site) after viewing only a single page.

What I have learned about social media may apply to you for becoming a recruiter attraction magnet.

## TWITTER, FACEBOOK, & INSTAGRAM

Although I feature a Twitter account on my website, I cannot connect the dots to my business value. I dip my toe in from time to time. I see colleagues repurposing items from their LinkedIn on Twitter, but those tweets appear to fall into a black hole with limited engagement. People either are ranting or being very PC (politically correct) on Twitter.

Facebook, for me, is an off and on relationship. I joined over a decade ago because an employee at Sprint was featuring her artwork on the site. I took an incognito approach, not accepting invites. I canceled my account some time back since I was not using it. Then a gastronomy need arose. While on my 2018 global explorer pursuits in Europe and the Caribbean, I needed to activate a new account for restaurant reservations since Yelp and OpenTable hadn't conquered the global marketplace. Then the Facebook account mothballed when Covid impacted my global travel bucket list. A renaissance transpired when I joined a book writing class in January 2021. It is where my instructor arrived live on Wednesdays, and my colleagues provided collaborative support. Since class ended in April 2021, I go to Facebook about once a month.

An Instagram button appears on my website, directing you to a mashup of my career consulting practice, travel pursuits, and gastronomy prefer-ences. I have two accounts: one for private usage with friends, another for business. The latter started in February 2019 when I launched my website. I became a passionate Canva design app user, creating my logo, marketing material, and social media posts. I only have a couple of clients connected with me on Instagram and two people direct messaged me for career consulting. Once again, not a place where my overall client base hangs out.

While my consulting clients do not find me on Facebook or Instagram, LinkedIn is my vetting ground for business introductions. Clients see my articles, virtual recommendations, work history, services summary, and contact information. Sometimes, clients message me through the LinkedIn platform Inmail or via my website contact form; there is the rare phone call or text.

## LINKEDIN SOCIAL SELLING INDEX

In November 2007, a CenturyLink colleague, Jeff Dennison, introduced me to LinkedIn. First, I was apprehensive about joining because I did not quite understand the business value for professional networking. Similar to the invitation-only Clubhouse, I thought, what value would this bring to my life? Remember the early days on LinkedIn when pop-ups barraged you for colleagues' skill endorsement requests like whack-a-mole?

LinkedIn's purpose changed when I was looking for a new career adventure after one too many Embarq and CenturyLink M&As. I hired a certified resume writer in Seattle and repurposed components for my LinkedIn profile. These two tools had recruiters contact me regarding technology marketing opportunities. After weighing external and internal job options, I stayed at CenturyLink but moved from marketing to an executive sales role, and LinkedIn took on a new meaning. LinkedIn became the way to connect my tech account base, prospects, channel partners, and share corporate resources. Then I retired, vanishing the LinkedIn need, or so I thought.

When I started my career consulting practice after post-retirement boredom, LinkedIn again became important. One-third of my business comes from LinkedIn balanced by client referrals and my website. My social imprint is money in the bank. That is why it should be important to you and your career. If you find a higher-paying role, you are accruing incremental investment income. Is it not easier to have recruiters come to you versus the other way around?

One way to view your professional image is by accessing the LinkedIn Sales Navigator at *www.linkedin.com/sales/ssi*. It features a free Social Selling Index (SSI) analysis based upon four components:

- **Establish your professional brand**: Complete your LinkedIn profile with the hiring manager or recruiter in mind. Become a thought-leader by publishing meaningful articles regarding your tech domain expertise.
- **Find the right people**: Identify potential network connections for your next tech role in less time using efficient search and research tools.
- **Engage with insights**: Discover and share

conversation-worthy updates to create and grow business relationships within your industry. Create posts and respond with comments to other colleagues' posts.

- **Build relationships**: Strengthen your professional network by finding and establishing trust with decision-makers. This builds a virtual network to replace the meet and greets of in-person industry trade shows and conferences.

In March 2021, my SSI was 68 out of 100, and when I checked again in August, it remained the same. My score reveals being in the top 9% of my LinkedIn network and top 26% within the Human Resources industry classification. My SSI changes based upon my weekly activity; spikes occur when I publish a post but not necessarily when I post articles. It is a strange phenomenon since articles take longer for me to develop than a random post. The LinkedIn algorithm throttles the distribution of posts, comments, and articles to your direct connections. Be forewarned that not all your relationships see what you post, or they receive a delayed appearance in their LinkedIn feed. I found that out a couple of months ago when a colleague's post hit my feed three days after he posted it.

## EXERCISE: PUT IT INTO PRACTICE

Please go to your worksheet for **Roadmap #3: Social Media Presence** and fill out the action plan.

**Action Plan**

1. Google your name and write down the top 5 results.
2. Does anything appear in your Google search that would raise an eyebrow to an executive recruiter? If so, consider deleting.
3. Access your LinkedIn Social Selling Index: Go to *www.linkedin.com/sales/ssi* and write down your results below.

a) Industry SSI Rank

b) Network SSI Rank

c) Current Social Selling Index

    i. Establish your personal brand

    ii. Find the right people

    iii. Engage with insights

    iv. Build relationships

d) People in your industry

e) People in your network

## KEY TAKEAWAYS

What is your bounce rate?

How you appear on social media can either put you in the executive search consideration set or diminish a terrific opportunity at another company seeking your skill sets. If you abandoned your Facebook page, have not looked at your Twitter feed, or neglected your LinkedIn profile, think of it as spring cleaning. Now is the time to conduct your annual social media performance reviews.

In this chapter on **Social Media,** you learned about:

- auditing your virtual presence,
- reviewing top professional branding outlets, and
- accessing your LinkedIn Social Selling Index score.

The next chapter will discuss sensitive subjects regarding your race, age, and gender.

# DIVERSITY & INCLUSION

I did not realize I was a prime target for a lawsuit. When I was a co-owner of a corporate brand consultancy, I wore many hats, including HR department. My business partner focused on business development projects with Brown-Forman, Coca-Cola, Frito-Lay, and General Motors, while simultaneously acting as the Dean of the Graduate School of Business at The University of Texas at Dallas.

The functions of recruiting, hiring, and, unfortunately, letting employees go fell squarely on my shoulders. I do not recall receiving an education specifically about human resources when I was in business school. Perhaps I glossed over it? Since I was in my 20s with zero experience working at a big-name corporation, I was on a steep learning curve in employee matters. There was not readily accessible information from the U.S. Equal Employment Opportunity Commission (EEOC) back then. I winged it and now cringe, thinking two people I had to let go because of non-performance might have sued my company.

Things changed when I joined Nortel Networks. At its peak during the tech bubble of 2000, Nortel reported about $30 billion in annual revenue and employed nearly 93,000 employees worldwide. I learned through our yearly HR compliance survey the do's and don'ts of employee and employer rights. When I was hiring staff at Nortel, I had a complete checklist of what I could ask with notations regarding unacceptable questions.

I reflect on my initial consulting and Nortel days when my clients voice their age, race, and gender concerns in the hiring process. There is bias out there and headline-making stories with ensuing lawsuits.

If you have focused little on diversity and inclusion, it is time to check your understanding of your legal rights and the corporation's policies. A recurring theme for executive clients seeking new roles is the desire for a collaborative and inclusive culture. My observation is that while some companies pay lip service to the notion, there is no real action behind the mission statement.

In this chapter, about **Diversity & Inclusion**, I will address how you should:

- counter the realities of bias and discrimination in job recruiting,
- evaluate a potential hiring company's point of view, and
- lead the charge for an inclusive workforce.

## AGE BIAS

When you are just entering the workplace, age hinders your opportunities for some jobs because companies are looking for experience. The proverbial Catch-22. On the other side of the curve, where my clients are, age may impact achieving your next role. Not a win-win? It does not have to be that way; it is time to take stock in your capabilities and experience.

According to the 2019 U.S. Census estimate, the median age is 38.4 within the 328 million population.[1] The older working-age population, ages 45 to 64, made up 26.4 percent.

Over 50 years ago, the Age Discrimination in Employment Act was made law, one of the premier statutes enforced by the U.S. Equal Employment Opportunity Commission (EEOC). I decided to review how this law came to be.

The 1965 Wirtz Report revealed "that employers believed age impacted ability. It also found that without any factual basis or consideration of individual abilities, employers routinely barred workers in their 40s, 50s, and 60s from a wide range of jobs."[2]

I have witnessed it personally for two clients who received abrupt endings to their 15-year corporate tenure. Shock and dismay sum up their situations after hearing about the elimination of their roles.

Ironically, you can be well past the retirement age of 65 and run a country; in the U.S. 2020 presidential election, there were two candidates in their 70s. Compare that to someone 50 years old, who is considered too old for a corporate role. Being considered too old for a job is not necessarily valid; however, it understandably raises strong emotions.

"How much of my career history should I share on my resume?" asked my client Jane. She was slightly concerned about how her 25 years of employment might take her out of the equation when applying for executive roles in IoT (Internet of Things), compared to younger candidates.

That is a fear I hear repeated by clients with long work histories at Microsoft, IBM, Intel, and Nike. They believe they will be passed over for the newer, shinier models; no doubt that sometimes happens. I witnessed it at Sprint and CenturyLink while reporting to leadership in the tongue-in-cheek "gifted and talented program." Don't get me wrong; some were gifted. The problem was that several leaders exhibited self-inflated righteousness. It is all about them, not the team. Do you know anyone who fits that description?

Depending how many companies and job positions clients have attained, I include 5 to 30 years of executive history. There is a discomfort with clients in their 40s and 50s regarding not sharing all of their job histories. I ease those concerns by addressing cumulative years starting at the director level in their resume summary. Companies hire you for your executive experience, not the software coding roles you held early on in your career. Yes, those early years built the foundation, but you probably don't want to jump into hands-on coding again. The biggest obstacle for my clients is editing career histories for highlights. I remind them that is why they hired me; I clean out their career history junk drawer.

Jane had an impressive 25-year career working for startups and ascending to a General Manager position at a top-ranked company. For her resume highlights, we settled on 14 years since that is where she started a director role before climbing to her current level. The result? The resume provided two pages of billion-dollar successes plus IoT and digital transformation industry awards recognition.

Fast forward to two months later. Jane sent me a note regarding an executive recruiting firm's request from a Japanese company they were representing. Before the job interview, they wanted her to provide her date of birth to validate her academic degrees, including a Bachelor of Science in Electrical Engineering and an MBA. She wanted to know my thoughts.

I thought it was peculiar requesting this before an actual job interview took place. Federal law does not prohibit employers from asking employees or job applicants about their age, typically appearing as a question on corporate job applications or through background checks. The Age Discrimination in Employment Act (ADEA) protects individuals by prohibiting discrimination against those age 40 and older. The question is, how do you remove the bias? Asking applicants for their date of birth might raise a red flag for how the company will use

the information. Jane was over 45, hence her appre-
hension.

I went into research mode. First, I checked out the
executive recruiting firm, a legitimate San Francisco-
based company with 500 employees. Next, I went to
LinkedIn to review the executive recruiter's impressive profile based on her career history and academic
foundation. Then I checked the profile of the
administrative assistant who was conducting this
request on behalf of the search firm. The admin's
background revealed she was not an HR expert and
strayed into an uncomfortable grey zone. My online
journey continued to understand Oregon state laws
regarding prospective employers asking about your
age before being offered a role.

In October 2020, I wrote a blog about ageism. Now
it was time to conduct Oregon-specific research on
employment law. Upon review, here is what I shared
with Jane:

> "Career interviewing is what I consider going
> on a business date. Why not see if you are
> interested in any of their positions before
> providing any information? You provide
> confidential details AFTER you have
> accepted the offer. Since you are not
> purchasing a home and placing an offer
> requiring a need to provide age and finan-
> cials, I would decline the request.

> "It is against the law in Oregon to ask for
> age. An employer—not a recruiter—can ask
> after you accepted an offer. You absolutely do

not have to provide. IMHO (in my humble opinion) they should understand HR law better."

While I was editing this chapter in August 2021, Jane sent me a follow-up email. Another Seattle-based executive search company had requested her birthdate for an academic background check before talking to a company they represented; she declined since she was pursuing two other opportunities. I asked a colleague about her thoughts, and she said if she was 35, no issue; otherwise, none of their business.

If you find yourself in the same quandary, my advice is to check out your local state employment rules. Based on what you find, you can suggest to the recruiter a preference for determining if the role is a good fit for both parties before giving out your date of birth or other information.

Negotiation is about knowing your rights. It is OK to question and say "no." On a related topic, I address the touchy salary question in the upcoming chapter about executive compensation. The fact is that over 50% of the states have enacted bans against asking salary history questions during a job interview.

## GENDER & SEXUAL ORIENTATION ISSUES

According to Title VII of the Civil Rights Act of 1965, "Sex discrimination involves treating someone (an applicant or employee) unfavorably because of that person's sex, including the person's sexual orientation, gender identity, or pregnancy." Even if there is a law, it still happens.

When I was in marketing roles, my hires tended to be females based upon their affinity for that career pathway. Although I also hired males, I did not really think about gender, since HR provided a list of talent available for my job postings across Kansas City, Dallas, and Reston, Virginia. That is why I can understand the female gender gap in tech engineering and computer roles. There is a larger pool of male talent receiving computer science and engineering degrees. The challenge is how to vet the best candidate without gender bias.

A 2020 Statista report highlights that women hold only 26.5% of executive, senior-level and management positions in S&P 500 companies, which is equivalent to many tech companies, but there is a wide gap in gender parity.[3] The report further notes that the female population at Microsoft is only 28%, while it almost doubles at Amazon at 42%. As a female, if the percentage is low, you can view this as an opportunity to make a difference in building a culture of inclusion; on the other hand, you may decide that this is not your tribe to join. I am fortunate to be acquainted with trailblazers at Amazon, IBM, Microsoft, and Nordstrom—male and female—who are chipping away at the gender divide through mentorship, coaching, and opportunities.

Have you noticed when a female fills a professional role for the first time, it generates a substantial amount of press? For example, U.S. Vice President

Kamala Harris. The question of belonging at a new company is one thing my female clients discuss with me. The reality is they, at times, are passed over for male candidates. If you look at the hiring company's executive team and it is predominantly male, this is a red flag or an opportunity for you to make a difference. Reach out to contacts at the hiring company and schedule a 15-minute call to understand their culture and if you would fit in.

Some of my clients identify as Lesbian, Gay, Bisexual, Transgender, and Queer (LGBTQ). On a consulting call, my client Lashawna discussed her hiring by a company who embraced her gender, sexual orientation, and racial identification. It is refreshing to hear when companies make hiring decisions on an inclusive basis. That is not always the case.

According to Catalyst Research, the population estimates for LGBTQ people are 4.5% in the U.S., 3% in Canada, 2.2% in the UK, and 10% in Japan.[4] In a 2021 research study of Fortune 500 companies, nondiscrimination policies that include sexual orientation fall below the 100% mark; 4% of the Fortune 500 are not beholden to these policies.

You can access a corporate website to check if they support an employee resource group or diversity council that includes LGBTQ and allied employees and programming. Once again, reach out to contacts at the hiring company and schedule a 15-minute call to discuss their culture of inclusion.

## RACIAL BIAS

Since I identify as a white female, I will never know what my non-white friends, clients, or colleagues experience with racial discrimination. My informal education arrived with them sharing their stories. Volunteering for Dress for Success, which supports all women regardless of race and age, I have heard testimony about obstacles related to the color of their skin or when English was a second language. I have not walked in their shoes and do not understand the full ramifications; however, I have seen the results. My education and admiration for those overcoming racial bias continues.

For example, I asked my client Ravi why he did not have a LinkedIn profile photo. His response: "Recruiters will not reach out to me because of my turban. I am concerned about discrimination."

After my jaw dropped, I told him, "When you get on a Zoom video, they will find out about your appearance. Why not rule out that type of company if they do not accept you for who you are?"

He had not thought of it that way.

Interviewing is a 2-way street; go where you match the culture. I am happy to say Ravi's profile now has a smiling turban-sporting avatar that looks fantastic! After three years at Facebook and 12 years at Microsoft, he landed a Director-level job at a $70MM-funded startup.

Thinking back, I had a similar discussion with a friend I met while volunteering; her name more or less identified her race. Closer to home, I had a family member who changed their last name to an Anglo-Saxon name with the rationale that it was easier to pronounce in Wall Street business dealings. It appears names are lightning rods for some people.

I am delighted to be married and gain the name of "Monique Montanino," since my maiden name was "Vrinds." Although spell check wants to make my former name "Friends."

It would be best to address whether you want to be a trailblazer at a company or opt-out of trying to push a boulder uphill.

## EVALUATING POTENTIAL COMPANY POV

I recommend talking to current employees regarding their views on the corporate culture. I did so last year when interviewing with a work transition company that reached out to me to join them as a contract coach. After searching their LinkedIn corporate profile, I identified a person in a similar role. Next, I dropped her a customized email acknowledging aspects of her background that resonated with me, requested a 15-minute call or Zoom, and provided five questions in advance. She responded within 24 hours, and we had the call, which helped me understand the corporate culture. It turns out I would not have been treated as a valued employee, more like an arm's-length hourly person. So, I decided not to pursue the opportunity. The days of working where I am not valued are in my rearview mirror.

Some companies, like Amazon, have entire sections of their website highlight all initiatives and indexes. Amin Shams, the former president of Glamazon, Amazon's affinity group for LGBTQ+, wrote in a March 2019 blog that Amazon attained a top score on the Human Rights Campaign's Corporate Equality Index. Further, the company scored 90/100 on the 2020 Disability Equality Index. Pique your interest?

Amazon conducted a global survey to arrive at their unique take on inclusion: "Being valued, trusted, connected, and informed so that we can deliver the best results for our customers."

There are several sites you can check for crowd-sourced opinions, such as Glassdoor and Fortune's *"100 Best Workplaces for Diversity."* In June 2021, I found a new site, Comparably, when checking out my former corporate alma mater, Lumen (previously CenturyLink). For diversity, Lumen ranks in the bottom 20% of companies with over 10,000 employees; this is based on a small sample size of 277 employees that rated the company 56/100 across various culture categories.

In summary, you benefit from getting continuous education regarding diversity and inclusion. Knowledge is power; do not be a lawsuit in the making like my former younger self. And seek a culturally diverse and inclusive tribe that will bring you joy. You deserve it!

## LEADING THE CHARGE OF INCLUSION

I believe that change for diversity, equity, and inclusion begins with each one of us. It is not just about liking a post on LinkedIn or Instagram; rather it is jumping into the fray and being part of the solution.

Last year, I attended a diversity and inclusion seminar sponsored by Dress for Success Austin for their volunteers. The goal was to raise awareness when interacting with clients; it was eye-opening for me. One of the topics addressed word choices and how patronizing specific phrases can be to women. We did not all feel the same way about words or questions among the female group of attendees. I guess that is the point; it is essential to obtain feedback, listen, and make changes.

## EXERCISE: PUT IT INTO PRACTICE

Please go to your worksheet for **Roadmap #3: Diversity & Inclusion** and fill out the action plan.

### Action Plan

1. Take a course: There are hundreds of free diversity and inclusion (D&I) virtual courses available. Coursera has one entitled *"Inclusive Leadership: The Power of Workplace Diversity"* that is offered by the University of Colorado.
2. Join a committee: Volunteer as a member of

your company's or a not-for-profit's D&I
committee.

3. Read a book: When I checked Amazon
online in August 2021, there were 745 books
available related to D&I; price certainly is
not a hurdle as some are free.

## KEY TAKEAWAYS

If you have stellar credentials or network connections—that it is how you land the job as an executive
—age, race, or gender may not tip the scales. When
you do not have connections to the companies you
are considering, bias can hinder your opportunities,
so the end-game is "become connected."

In this chapter about **Diversity & Inclusion**, you
learned about:

- countering the realities of bias and
  discrimination in job recruiting,
- evaluating a potential hiring company's
  point of view, and
- leading the charge for an inclusive
  workforce.

Congratulations, you have completed the third point
on your career success roadmap for **Personal
Branding**!

Now, you are in the driver's seat for your personal
brand because your knowledge base grew to:

- determine your superpower,

- identify your top leadership and technical skills,
- create your impactful introductory elevator pitch,
- harness your social media impact, and
- address ageism, diversity, and gender bias.

In the next section, we discuss your career curb appeal. How do you show up on a resume or LinkedIn profile? Or in an interviewing environment?

## Career Roadmap Point #4
# Job Search Tools

Now we will conduct a deep dive into best practices for **Job Search Tools** on the fourth point of your 5-step roadmap. In your tech job search, you are probably curious about where the most prominent opportunities reside.

According to the U.S. Bureau of Labor & Statistics: "Employment of computer and information technology occupations is projected to grow 11 percent from 2019 to 2029. These occupations are projected to add about 557,100 new jobs."[1]

That is more than half a million jobs in a decade being driven by cloud computing, collection and storage of big data, and information security. The report summarizes the top five positions ranked in order of the highest salary:

- Computer & information research scientists
- Computer network architects
- Software developers, quality assurance analysts, and testers
- Information security analysts

- Database administrators

When I checked LinkedIn in August 2021, there were over 35,400 U.S. job postings for technology executives. However, perusing the list, not all had what I consider a C-Suite or executive leadership title. The job pool narrows when applying specific labels such as tech CEO, which resulted in 738 listings, or tech CIO with 117 results.

While the opportunities within the tech industry are significant, becoming an executive is a challenge, since not all positions appear online. It is a secret society that you may join if you make a concerted effort to tap it; it is probably a reason you bought this book.

After conducting more than 1,350 resume critiques, 700 coaching sessions, and 350 LinkedIn makeovers, I am savvy about being a recruiter magnet. For example, my client Lakshmi landed a Director-level role at Amazon after 19 years at IBM in part due to our interviewing practice, but the true foundation is how awesome she is.

Same experience for Thomas—after 13 years at Microsoft, he landed a leadership position at Amazon but then parlayed it into an equity position with a startup three months later.

At this fourth roadmap point, I will share my career consulting best practices and industry research related to your **Job Search** touching upon:

- executive resumes,
- LinkedIn profiles,
- interviews, and
- executive compensation.

# EXECUTIVE RESUME

Does your resume have cobwebs, and it is time to contact pest control? You are in luck since we will dive into the modern standard for garnering interest from executive recruiters in this chapter. There is a large amount of advice on resumes backed up by the 9.8 billion results appearing when I googled it.

In this chapter, about the **Executive Resume**, I will walk through:

- creating a resume from scratch,
- using Applicant Tracking System (ATS) software, grammar, and spelling apps, and
- writing a cover letter or introductory email.

The National Résumé Writers' Association (NRWA) has a 50-page style guide I use as a baseline to create executive resumes. Your resume's purpose is to capture attention, generate interest, create desire, and inspire action by a hiring manager or recruiter. The guide covers nine topics:

- Plan your writing strategy
- Professional summary and headline
- Professional experience
- Optional sections
- Grammar overview
- Formatting and design
- Cover letters (spoiler alert, yes, you need one to stand out)
- Electronic documents and ATS
- Final submission: Proofreading and editing

If you are a resume DIY (do it yourself) type of person, I will provide highlights from each of the above sections for your resume update. For the rest of you planning to hire a resume writer, this will explain how the components are generated.

For your writing strategy, it starts with the position you are seeking. I typically review three job postings online and run a client's resume through an ATS application. As I mentioned in the Superpower chapter, I use Jobscan, which you can access by visiting *www.jobscan.co*. That is not a typo at the end of the domain; it is "co" versus "com." The Jobscan ATS output identifies format issues and highlights hard and soft skills related to the job posting. I transfer the analysis into an Excel spreadsheet and then note the skills that appear multiple times across all the three jobs. These are the top keywords for crafting a resume to optimize your tech skills and experiences.

Here is a trick about ATS—it will not read anything that appears in your header or footer, so I create the resume masthead within the body of the Word document for the client's name, city, state, phone, email, and LinkedIn URL. Due to industry HR privacy concerns, your numbered street address should not appear.

Next, I create a headline such as "Chief Technology Officer" with three sub-components like "cloud computing, software engineering, and distributed systems." For the professional summary, I develop four power statements with facts and figures to win a favorable impression within 15 seconds. Professional summaries should not be written in the third person. Delete pronouns along with articles (e.g., "I," "the," "a") to enhance your white space for readability; it is all about the highlights reel.

The professional experience section contains four essential components: 1) company information with a brief description, 2) job position title, 3) dates right-adjusted unless work gaps, and 4) job description punctuated by a period. Each job role lists 2-5 bullets containing metrics (e.g., increased market share by 10%, drove annual revenue by $10MM, improved customer satisfaction by 5%, hired 60 staff members in three months). If there is not a metric, frankly, no one cares since it is not grounded in a fact. Think about when you purchase something on Amazon; I read the 5-star reviews, so apply the same logic here to establish why you would be an excellent hire.

Optional sections cover professional certifications, continuing professional education, professional associations, and volunteer activities.

For grammar, proofreading, and editing, I pay a subscription fee for the Grammarly app, although they offer a free and less robust option. The NWRA guide adheres to the grammar and punctuation standards in *The Greg Reference Manual* and *Webster's Dictionary*—the same dictionary my mother bought me at 11 years old, so I have come full circle.

In formatting, the resume standard strives for a clean and concise end product. Some people want their resume to pop with graphics; once again, ATS cannot read text within illustrations, so I do not include charts unless you plan to send it directly to a hiring manager. The standard calls for sans serif fonts such as Arial or Calibri with a minimum 10-size font and the use of only 1-2 colors, with black being the selection for your text.

Resumes come across my computer with tiny margins when clients attempt to dump their career junk drawer into 2-3 pages. My standard is 1-inch left/right and top/bottom while the NCRW guide allows ½-inch wide. The recommendation is to vary line spacing between position descriptions and bulleted statements to avoid dense paragraphs of five lines. Since I became certified in Information Mapping while at Sprint, I advise you to list skills below your professional summary in alphabetical order for the reader to search for specific ones readily versus what you think is a top skill. The idea is to provide simple breadcrumbs to attract views.

After I proofread the first draft, I run it through ATS again and tweak it for each client's job postings. Then I review with my client and finalize the edits to yield the master resume of 2-3 pages. In reality, no one ever reads the second page except to check on your education.

## COVER LETTERS

Cover letters are a hotly debated topic for job searching. While volunteering as a career consultant at Dress for Success in Seattle, my client and I discussed cover letters. She was not a fan, and then one of my volunteer colleagues, a former client, chimed in, stating she abhorred them. We spent three minutes discussing the pros and cons.

The Ladders' analysis of 300 job postings for tech giants, medium-sized companies, and fast-growing startups revealed that more than half the tech companies (56%) still add the cover letter fields to their application forms.[1]

As a business owner and former Fortune 500 hiring manager, receiving a cover letter made a positive impression when a candidate profoundly stated their case to be hired.

Think about it. If you received 100 resumes for a position, beyond the basics of academics and skills, what would stand out for you regarding potential employees? I would venture to say focused interest, conviction, and passion will shine through.

There are compelling reasons for submitting cover letters. A tailored cover letter can provide specifics for why you are interested in joining a company (e.g., incredible technology, market share growth, inclusive culture) and what you are like to work with from a personality and leadership perspective. Further, you can explain why you are leaving your current role and your value to the hiring company.

My clientele derives from different sources, including my websites, LinkedIn Pro, referrals, and networking. I always send proposals, and when we agree to collaborate, I ask what the selection criteria were. Overwhelmingly, it was because I customized my note after researching my client's career, accomplishments, skill sets, and their colleagues' recommendations on LinkedIn. My proposal is my consulting cover letter for one-on-one job consultations. In a nutshell, I understand your value and can enhance your brand, enabling you to apply for a position, interview confidently, and get a job offer. The bottom line: you select people based upon mutual considerations.

**Cons**

- **Time Consuming**: It takes time to find corporate information regarding address, hiring manager, and providing why you are the perfect candidate for the job. Yes, I spend an hour researching and writing a cover letter for a specific client opportunity because a $10K-$100K benefit package increase is worth the investment. Or, sometimes, a job is worth it after a layoff or sabbatical.
- **Recruiter's Disinterest**: My colleague

told me that some job postings don't require it, so why bother? My retort was that you can't know what a recruiter will think. Just because the recruiter is disinterested does not mean a targeted cover letter to the VP or CxO will not find its way to them. When I was a Sprint hiring manager, the little things differentiated candidates, with a cover letter being one of them for granting an interview.

## Pros

- **Personal Branding**: A cover letter allows you to reinforce your brand, provide evidence for why you will make an impact, and differentiate yourself from other potential candidates. It will enable you to toot your own horn.
- **Positive Impression**: Researching a company, its leadership, mission, and accomplishments, provides the opportunity to state why you want to be employed there and add value. How would you feel if someone showed up knowing your business accomplishments and challenges and offered thoughts on innovation for a positive impact? The cover letter allows you to deliver that message.
- **Differentiator**: An Amazon executive questioned whether cover letters made a difference. After customizing a message for him for a targeted position, he had an *"aha"* moment. It was his story stated in the first

person. Contrary to a resume, cover letters show your responsibilities and accomplishments customized in your personal voice to the open job requisition. You are unique; here is your opportunity to report your vision, leadership style, and successes with a personal perspective that will resonate with the hiring CEO or recruiter.

## WHAT WOULD A TECH EXEC DO?

My technology executive clients hire me for career strategy and personal branding. Guess what? They almost always request a cover letter or email intro. Why? They want the competitive edge to position themselves for the job as a differentiator. It is branding and has a monetary valuation. If executives who are earning $200K-$1MM in compensation create cover letters, you should too.

I provide customized templates for my clients with the following components:

- **Your Contact Info**: Provide your name, only city and state (no address because of corporate privacy concerns), phone number, and LinkedIn URL. And, yes, anyone can google you and find out your physical address, unless you are in the witness protection program, but that is not the point. Job in Seattle, you live in Seattle, one check mark for the hiring company not needing to pay for a relocation.

- **Addressee**: If you do not know who the hiring manager is, find a person to address your letter by uncovering the firm's top technologist or HR executive. The same goes for the mailing address by researching corporate headquarters or local address. These days, we email, but the effort to uncover the details shows your interest and commitment.
- **Introduction**: Begin the first sentence with your years of experience and industry expertise using keywords from the job description. Detail the position title and company name for reader focus, especially for an executive search firm or recruiting agency. Explain a pivotal differentiator to capture why the reader should continue. This is your hook to the recruiter. One client has made a billion-customer impact. I'm all in to read more about her, how about you?
- **Company Focus**: Provide a sentence regarding what resonates with you about the company's culture, mission, or product. The subsequent sentence should outline what company accomplishments impress you from market share, innovation, or industry disruption. This section shows your research investment and understanding of their big picture and why you will align.
- **Your Brand**: The last paragraph before closing is a bulleted list of three interpersonal and industry skills you can bring to the table. Why should the company

hire you? For my culinary aficionados, what is your secret sauce? Tech executive positions are looking for cross-functional team leadership, strategic planning, operational excellence, technical innovation, and a coaching component. For each of the skills, create a metric-based anecdote to back it up.

- **The Close**: Thank them for their consideration and note your contact information if it is not at the top of your cover letter.

## EXERCISE: PUT IT INTO PRACTICE

Please go to your worksheet for **Roadmap #4: Executive Resume** and fill out the action plan.

### Action Plan

1. Resume & Cover Letter Analysis: If you google free resume analysis, you will find several companies that offer it. This analysis is a simple way to see what gaps, if any, exist. Be forewarned that everything looks like a nail when you are a hammer, so a resume company reviewer will definitely find issues.

2. DIY: If you have the time, you certainly can create or optimize your resume. If you decide to go with this approach, find a layout that is ATS compatible. I have samples on my website *www.resumetech.guru*.

3. Hire a Professional: I did competitive research to determine my resume pricing.

You can expect to pay anywhere from $500 to $3,000 for a technology executive resume. LinkedIn is a starting point to search for a resume writer. Or better yet, call me!

## KEY TAKEAWAYS

It's all about your career curb appeal. Now you have a general understanding of how ATS operates to keep the job search bots (software programs that perform automated tasks) and recruiters intrigued. A resume plus a corresponding tailored cover letter or introductory email are the door openers for recruiters and hiring managers.

In this chapter, about the **Executive Resume**, you learned about:

- creating a resume from scratch,
- using ATS software, grammar, and spelling apps, and
- writing a cover letter or introductory email.

In the next chapter, we will tackle optimizing your LinkedIn profile to become an online click magnet.

# LINKEDIN PROFILE

Microsoft's biggest acquisition in 2016 was LinkedIn, purchased for $26.2 billion. It was Satya Nadella's first major acquisition as CEO, and he viewed the professional networking site as a way for people to find jobs, build skills, sell, market, and get work done. At that time, there were 433 million LinkedIn members compared to 1.2 billion Microsoft Office users. Fast forward to five years later, LinkedIn membership grew 78%, with over 774 million users in more than 200 countries and territories in 2021. It is here to stay.

I recall a humorous and intriguing post on LinkedIn. A 2017 Microsoft study found that the average human attention span is 8 seconds versus 12 seconds highlighted in the original 2000 analysis. Further, the study's researchers claim that the human attention span is now less than a goldfish. This silly factoid captured my attention since I recall my first date with my husband in a Dallas restaurant featuring goldfish suspended in fishbowls above the bar. I asked the bartender how often they replaced the goldfish; weekly was the response. The punch-line is goldfish may have a greater attention span than humans, but it is short-lived.

Got your attention? Great, now let us talk about how LinkedIn can either drive or diminish your chances based on an 8-9 second delay depending on how you classify yourself: human or goldfish. There are many creative LinkedIn hacks ensuring you will be found by executive recruiters and hiring managers.

In this chapter, about the **LinkedIn Profile**, I will discuss how to:

- review the five major components of your profile,
- optimize for viewer click rates, and
- target executive recruiters.

A standard comment from my clients, who never really had to apply for a job working at Microsoft or IBM, is that their LinkedIn profile needs life support. My experience is quite different since I estimate that over 25% of my professional time evolves around LinkedIn: optimizing it for clients, using it for communication and industry learning. For a 30-minute to a 1-hour investment of your time, it is easy to pump life back into your LinkedIn profile in five easy steps.

## 5 MAJOR COMPONENTS

Are you an *"All-Star"*? I am not talking about Major League Baseball, but your LinkedIn online presence. It is easy to find out by accessing your profile to see how you fit on the novice-to-expert continuum: *Beginner*, *Intermediate*, *Advanced*, *Expert*, and *All-Star*. Your status appears on your LinkedIn dashboard, which appears as the second significant section on your profile.

If you uploaded a profile photo, have 50 connections, and filled out these five sections, you are a LinkedIn *All-Star*:

- Headline
- About
- Industry & location
- Experience
- Education

The most compelling reason for an *All-Star* profile is that 1.6 million engaged talent professionals—recruiters and hiring managers—use LinkedIn. You will gain a competitive advantage among millions of LinkedIn members if you have an *All-Star* profile. When looking for candidates, recruiters access over 40 advanced filters, using keyword or Boolean search, based on LinkedIn signals, such as "open to work."

LinkedIn factors into a sizable part of job recruitment efforts with more than 57 million companies listed on the site and 13 million job opportunities.[1]

The other use for an *All-Star* profile is when you apply for a job, since companies connect their Applicant Tracking System (ATS) with LinkedIn Recruiter. Over 90% of the Fortune 500 companies use ATS to scan resumes and 75% of candidates are removed from consideration, based on low job qualification scores.[2]

When in doubt, the Jobscan app, discussed previously, not only tells you which ATS is scoring your resume against the job posting but provides tips for resume input.

The top five ATS used by enterprise and mid-market companies are Workday, Taleo (by Oracle), Success-Factors (by SAP), iCIMS, and Greenhouse.[3] There are 28 standard ATS systems listed on LinkedIn, while additional ones can connect, including Microsoft's proprietary system.

- Adapt, ADP, Avature
- Bullhorn, Bullhorn Connexys, Bull Jobscience, Bullhorn for Salesforce
- ClearCompany, cornerstone
- Dynamics ATS
- erecruit
- Greenhouse
- Haufe
- iCIMS
- JazzHR, JobAdder, JobDiva, Jobscore, Jobvite
- Lever
- Mercury xRM
- PageUp

- Saba Lumesse, SmartRecruiters
- Taleo, Teamtailor
- Workable, Workday

## PHOTOS

There is a reason real estate agents feature photos on their business cards and ads; it is all about branding. Agents are in the people business to sell homes, so an image reveals several things to a home buyer such as trust, style, success, gender, and age. I know people who are not comfortable sharing a photo online, but LinkedIn statistics reveal you will garner more recruiter engagement with 21 times more profile views and nine times more connection requests.[4] It does not pay to appear as a "ghost" or be in the witness protection program when trying to become a recruiter magnet.

Here are my client recommendations for LinkedIn headshots and background photos:

- **Headshot:** It is time to update your headshot if it is more than five years old. Professional photographers charge between $250-$500 with options to meet in a studio or location. An alternative is to have someone take a new photo with a non-busy background. For the best results, professionals recommend dawn or dusk for the best light. I updated my headshot in September 2021 and met the photographer in the morning at my choice of the Olympic

Sculpture Park in downtown Seattle. Studies indicate we do not select our best photos, so I asked for client feedback. Another option to consider is using a data science-backed analysis such as *www.photofeeler.com*. This app provides crowdsourced business profile ratings based upon how competent, likable, and influential you appear in the photo.

- **Background Photo**: Think of this as personal brand real estate to highlight your unique background. You can update your background photo with a copyright-free photo from *www.unsplash.com* or *www.pexels.com*. Another idea is to take an image related to your regional area, like the downtown Seattle skyline with the Space Needle or interests such as kite surfing.

## HEADLINE

I develop headlines for my clients with three components in mind, including an industry title, domain expertise, and differentiator. In between the components, I insert separator symbols such as the pipe which appears as the vertical line key (|), or Unicode bullets (squares and circles).

As far as an industry-recognized title, that is easy to discover by conducting a LinkedIn job search. For example, while searching for a Fortune 100 client role in the U.S., "Chief Information Officer" provided 2 times (4,000) more job postings than "CIO" at 2,000. Or you can include both: "Chief Information Officer (CIO)."

LinkedIn lacks the capability to bold, italicize, or underline. If you want to bold your headline, you can use a free text formatter which translates into Unicode bullets. I use the resource at *www.linked-makeover.com/linkedin-text-formatter*.

## ABOUT (AKA THE SUMMARY)

Think of this section as your elevator pitch when the recruiter asks, "So, tell me about yourself." My advice is to respond from a position of strength. Explain what you do, and your philosophy regarding leading successful teams and achieving incredible results.

Most people in their LinkedIn "About" section write about themselves in the third person. That is uber weird. It is your profile, not an introduction at a keynote presentation. Let's turn that around and position yourself for the next executive role you want. When you are hiring someone, what impresses you in the interview? It is time to interview yourself or phone a colleague for your summary.

One of my favorite summaries has a line that caught my attention and made me smile: "Leader with a talent for driving strategic relationships with clients and finding mutual wins in complex negotiations. I have negotiated with terrorists; executives do not intimidate me." Kudos to Matt Keyes!

Matt is a former sales executive colleague at Centu-ryLink. So please follow his lead: Do more of that. We are here to be dazzled, not bored.

## SKILLS

For ATS optimization, add updates to your LinkedIn skills section. The limit is 50 skills, so if you max out, delete current skills with zero endorsements or insignificant items related to your next role regardless of a high endorsement count. Prioritize industry terminology that recruiters use instead of internal corporate babble and acronyms no one understands. What AWS discusses in meetings might be the same as Microsoft but within different vernaculars, so cover all your bases.

There are four skills categories:

- Industry Knowledge
- Tools & Technologies
- Interpersonal Skills
- Other Skills

As an executive, I recommend focusing on interpersonal skills. In my review of thousands of job postings, recurring top skills are leadership, mentoring, coaching, diversity and inclusion, innovation, negotiation, problem-solving, strategic direction, and vision.

Did you know the top three skills in your profile rank in quantitative order, and you can change them to reflect your strengths for your next role?

- Click the Me icon at the top of your LinkedIn homepage.
- Click View Profile.

- Scroll down to the Skills & Endo.
  section and click the Edit icon.
- In the pop-up window, click and drag t.
  Reorder icon (four horizontal bars), locate
  to the right of the corresponding skill you'd
  like to move.

If your interpersonal skill counts are low, reach out to colleagues to request endorsements and detail the specific items. It is an efficient way to increase your skill rankings when necessary.

## RECOMMENDATIONS

I know it is sometimes challenging to ask for help but get over it. No one that I know can do everything themselves. It is OK to receive LinkedIn recommendations; you have earned those.

I tell my clients when requesting recommendations to be extremely specific about a skill they want to highlight. The ones like "he/she is a nice person" do not convey to a recruiter or hiring manager what executive leadership strengths you possess. Request recommendations for leadership qualities:

- Strong vision for the future
- Ability to establish trust
- Leadership style that reflects your team
- Delegation to your direct reporting managers
- Mentor capabilities for the development team

Being a master communicator
- Inspiring a team to accomplish great work

Here are the steps to take to request a recommendation from your profile:

- Click the Me icon at the top of your LinkedIn homepage.
- Select View Profile. Scroll down to the Recommendations section.
- Click Ask for a recommendation.
- Type the name of the connection you'd like to ask for a recommendation in the "who do you want to ask?" box.

## COMPETITION

Although not part of the *All-Star* profile, you can turn off a setting to stop highlighting your competition to recruiters. You heard that right. It is like when you shop on Amazon and on the bottom it says, "since you viewed this product, you might be interested in this." Why make it easy for recruiters to leave your profile and go on to someone similar?

- The People Also Viewed box shows other profiles that viewers of a LinkedIn profile have looked at—your competition. You may see it on your profile or someone else's profile. You can show or hide this feature from your profile through your Settings & Privacy page.
- Click the Me icon at the top of your LinkedIn homepage.

- Click Settings & Privacy.
- Click the Account preferences section c the left rail.
- Click Change next to Viewers of this profile also viewed.
- Toggle to the left or right to select No or Yes, respectively.
- Changes will be saved automatically.

## RECRUITER OPEN TO NETWORK

Armed with your *All-Star* profile, you are now ready to notify recruiters you are open to being contacted. Yes, you will initially receive some odd "does not even vaguely represent me" requests but give it a whirl.

Here is how you tell recruiters you are available without letting your network or boss know.

- Click on the Open To dropdown that appears below your photo on the left-hand side.
- Select finding a new job.
- Add four job titles; that is the maximum.
- Add locations; you can click on the box underneath and select I am open to remote work.
- Choose who sees you are open to work, select "recruiters only," then add it to your profile.

For the four job titles, as I mentioned in the head-line creation section, you can conduct a LinkedIn job search based on various job titles to see how many openings exist within your geography and rank order. For example, for a Fortune 100 General Manager, I uncovered the following in July 2021. It is noticeable that a Chief Information Officer generates almost twice as many LinkedIn job listings as a CIO. That is crowdsourced information by the HR departments or recruiters who designated the titles for the job openings, so I recommend starting with the highest job count.

### Title | LinkedIn U.S. Job Counts

Chief Information Officer | 4,050
Chief Technology Officer | 3,651
CIO | 2,003
CTO | 1,764

## EXERCISE: PUT IT INTO PRACTICE

Please go to your worksheet for **Roadmap #4: LinkedIn Profile** and fill out the action plan for your *All-Star* profile. LinkedIn awards extra credit if you follow the steps outlined in this chapter for photos, headlines, skills, recommendations, competition, and recruiter open to network suggestions.

### Action Plan

Before steamrolling ahead on your LinkedIn updates, let's do a safety check so your professional network and boss won't raise an eyebrow. Avoid the embarrassment of a client who did not follow this protocol; his network commented with hearty congratulations on a new role at Microsoft when in fact he only had tweaked his title to become more marketable to recruiters. Awkward.

1. Safety Check

> a) Profile Update: Turn Off Notifications.
> b) Click the Me icon in the top right corner of your LinkedIn homepage.
> c) Select Settings & Privacy from the dropdown.
> d) Click on Visibility, then Visibility of your LinkedIn activity.
> e) Select Share profile updates with your network and confirm No. If not, toggle to the left for No.

2. Photo: Upload a professionally styled photo taken recently with an engaging smile.

3. Headline: Include the title of your next role in ATS terminology, your domain expertise, and your key differentiator from the other four executives vying for the same job.

4. About: Write a first-person elevator pitch that highlights your years of executive experience and domain expertise and that tells an engaging story.

5. Industry & location: If you live in a suburban or rural area, I suggest adding the closest metropolitan area. For example, I choose Greater Seattle area, instead of Redmond, Washington, for Microsoft clients.

6. Experience: The rule of thumb is to list job roles for the past 10-15 years since technology changes. It does not have to start with your first job out of college. For each job, write a sentence incorporating key responsibilities, followed by 1-2 bullets featuring a strategic accomplishment as a metric (e.g., decreased operating expenses by 15%; increased cloud consumption by $5 million annually; and managed a global cross-functional technology team of 500.)

7. Education: As an executive, where you went to high school is irrelevant, so delete. The Bachelors, Masters, or Ph.D. are what recruiters are seeking.

## Key Takeaways

People have an 8-second attention span. Do you have an excellent profile that will cause an executive recruiter to send you a text for a meeting? Fix your gaps and make it happen!

If you desire better vetting and increased viewership by recruiters and hiring managers, it is time to look at your LinkedIn profile with a highly critical eye. It may be time-consuming, but updating your LinkedIn profile is your opportunity to build your online brand for your career curb appeal.

In this chapter, about the **LinkedIn Profile**, you learned about:

- reviewing the five major components of your existing profile,

- optimizing for viewer click rates, and
- targeting executive recruiters.

In the next chapter, you will learn the Amazon magic for perfecting your interviewing skills. It is all in the STAR.

# MASTER THE INTERVIEW

Are you ready for your close-up? How much difference a year makes with the need to be camera-ready during the continuing Covid crisis. A Gartner survey indicates 86% of companies are conducting virtual interviews to hire candidates.[1] Unfortunately, not everyone is a natural for interviews, even in person, so the video component may add an extra burden. For example, Sheryl, a director at Microsoft, contacted me about preparing for an internal job interview.

With 17 years of experience at the same company, she surprised me when she said, "I bombed during the last interview for another internal job opening several months ago. Even though I knew the hiring VP, the questions she asked caught me off guard. For this new opportunity, I want to prepare for the upcoming interviewing panel."

I reviewed the job requisition, checked out the domain industry trends, and scanned the hiring manager's LinkedIn profile. I sent Sheryl a list of nine questions to prepare for our video interviewing role play session.

During the Q&A session, I asked all the questions and then sprang this one on her: "Tell me about a time you disagreed with a colleague. What is the process you used to work it out?"

She blurted out, "Hey, that's not fair; it wasn't one of the questions you sent me."

To which I responded, "Well, you are not going to know what the interviewing panel will ask either. It is best to have a plan on how to respond to any type of question."

A 2020 remote hiring research study revealed that most candidates who did not land a job offer were distracted during the interview, did not engage with the recruiter, or appeared to be reading from a script.[2]

I noticed Sheryl was reading from a script, since she had written responses to all of my nine questions. It came across as inauthentic, which is far from the type of person she is. We spent the next 15 minutes working out a plan so she would not be caught unprepared.

In this chapter, about how to **Master the Interview**, I will:

- cover your elevator pitch,
- review behavioral questions and technical knowledge,
- eliminate the jitters, and

- advise on thank you notes.

Over the past three years, I have reviewed research studies, searched publications, and followed career experts' advice regarding best practices for job interviews. A sizable portion of my consulting focuses on clients mastering the interview. It prompted me to develop a four-page interviewing guide, which we will use in this chapter.

## ELEVATOR PITCH REVISITED

The first question any recruiter or hiring manager asks is the infamous "so, tell me about yourself." If you recall, in the **Personal Branding** section of this book, I outlined the answering components to boost confidence during delivery. It is such a critical part of your brand that it is definitely worth a revisit.

I believe in the simplicity of three parts for answering an interview question.

- **Who**: Explain who you are from a career perspective.
- **Evidence**: Place your experience into context and use a statistic or quantifiable measurement.
- **Results**: Highlight intangible strengths you deliver to a hiring company.

Once again, here is my elevator pitch to clients.

"I have arrived full circle from corporate

brand consulting at Coca-Cola, General Motors, and the U.S. Army to personal brand consulting for technology executives. After 18 years as a marketing and sales executive at Fortune 500 companies, I retired early four years ago. I got bored, became a volunteer career advocate, and my former colleagues mentioned they would pay me for help on their resumes and LinkedIn profiles. My personal brand consulting practice for technology executives was born."

You will notice it is not a laundry list of skills or a deep dive into how long I worked at a company. My former consulting customers are what I think of as hearing candy to a prospective client, but I never even listed the companies I worked for—Sprint and CenturyLink. I did not talk about working for the now-defunct billion-dollar Nortel Networks. It is a simple story of how I started, where I am now, and my benefits to a client.

My suggestion: Be innovative and play with it. I wrote a pitch for a client related to his hobby of cycling.

"I am all about endurance and embracing the adventure. Earlier this year, I spent my 3-month sabbatical after years with <company> cycling from Washington state down the Pacific Coast Highway to Palm Springs.

"On a long hill or mountain pass, those seemingly endless climbs test the strongest.

Keeping a tenacious, positive mindset makes a big difference. I used the same approach to deliver technology innovation, operations, and cross-functional initiatives at <company>. It was a pleasure to join <company> as an initial startup and support the IPO, which led to the $8.3 billion acquisition."

Let's unpack this story: adventure, sabbatical, and billion-dollar outcome. Make your response a personal tale; recruiters lean in, so try it!

## INTERVIEW Q&A

I use a modified version of the Amazon STAR (situation, tasks, actions, results) method for storytelling. Based on my affinity for 3-part answers, I developed the CAR (context, actions, results).

Amazon is proactive in their interviewing process, sending candidates a 2-page phone interview preparation document. It breaks down their STAR method, general interview tips, and leadership principles. With all that terrific information, you would think most candidates would be well prepared, but, alas, it is not the case. Some of my clients are pretty simply inadequate at interviewing. They either under- or over-prepare and are full of anxiety. Good news, there is a fix.

Here is what I advise for your job interview Q&A.

- **Stories**: Prepare six phenomenal stories related to your leadership, team building, innovation, problem-solving, biggest

mistake, and differentiators. Write them out
with a 3-part answer in mind. What is the
context of the story, your actions, and the
ultimate result?

- **Potential Interviewer Questions**: If you
google Amazon interviewing questions, you
will find a plethora of responses. I watched
countless YouTube videos related to
interviews and generated a master list of
questions based on the 14 leadership
principles. It is a terrific foundation for
what any company may ask. It is based
upon: 1) customer obsession, 2) ownership,
3) invent and simplify, 4) are right, a lot; 5)
learn and be curious, 6) hire and develop the
best, 7) insist on the highest standards, 8)
think big, 9) a bias for action, 10) frugality,
11) earn trust, 12) dive deep, have backbone;
13) disagree and commit, and 14) deliver
results. Once again, have a 3-part answer.
- **Timing**: A client interviewing for AWS
needed to develop 5-minute answers,
including the month and year of a project.
Talk about detail. For a client's panel
preparation, we practiced 1-minute and 5-
minute in-depth responses. The best way to
practice is to record yourself on your phone
or computer with Microsoft Teams, WebEx,
or Zoom. It seems awkward at first, but
then you will optimize your response.
- **Your Questions**: Since an interview is a 2-
way street, prepare a list of 5-10 questions.
Indeed, some are answered during your
discussion, but the proverbial prompt for

your questions is always at the end. In my four-page interviewing guide, I created questions for clients: a) How has consumer behavior changed during the pandemic? b) Could you describe your management style and the type of employee that works well with you? c) At the end of the year, how would you know you hired the right person? d) How would you rate the company's progress on diversity and inclusion? e) What are the most significant opportunities facing the company? f) What drew you to working for the company? g) Can you tell me about the team I will be leading? h) Do you have any hesitations about my qualifications?

## JITTER-FREE

It is all in the preparation, but over-preparation causes problems too. Shake it off, take a deep breath, and embrace a mutually beneficial conversation for your interview.

- **Research**: Go to the company's website and uncover their mission and whether it resonates with your life's purpose. You will spend a minimum of 60 hours per week at a desk or inside your brain focusing on the company's directives. Is this a good fit for you? For their financials, you need to determine if they are a sound investment for your future. There are several companies out there who make the news, but their financials are terrible. For example, someone on LinkedIn was extolling the virtue of WeWork. In 2018, their revenue increased to $1.8 billion from $886 million in the prior year, but over that same stretch, its net loss more than doubled to $1.9 billion. Beyond financials, in the rare chance you get to interview in person, will they be a company worth your values, ideas, and energy? And beyond that, do they have a nice lobby? I give credit to Nigel Dessau. His tweet had me in stitches: "I am once again reminded that the lobby of your office = the culture inside." No kidding. Thank goodness my clients did not want to meet me at my former $23 billion company office in downtown Seattle. The conference room had a spectacular view, but the office consisted of mismatched, antiquated equipment, stained chairs, and carpet augmented by a dingy hospital ward atmosphere. Not good; nowhere near good.

- **Practice**: Write down your stories with the 3-part rule; then practice those. When I did my 5-minute book debut in April 2021, I wrote an elevator pitch and read an excerpt from my book. For two weeks on my daily walks, I practiced my five minutes out loud while walking around Austin's Lady Bird Lake. Next, I recorded myself three times. With practice, I improved to meet the 5-minute constraint.

- **Know your audience:** My clients and I collaborate on researching their potential employers by checking out the company's website for basic facts like their mission, strategy, and financial performance. We read about the interview panel participants on LinkedIn, in the news, and on their blogs. This is business intelligence in its best form; the interviewer will appreciate knowing you took the time to learn about their background. It builds a bridge if done right.

- **Anticipate interview questions**: Teaming with my clients, I created a 1-page position sheet to prepare for the interview. We develop questions to be answered or asked. The latter includes questions to the interviewer regarding: a) What drew you to working here? b) What is a typical day? c) How can I succeed to the next level at the company? and d) What can I accomplish within the role that will make me the best hiring decision for you?

- **Dress accordingly:** We are grown adults; well, most of us. For the interview, I dress conservatively, whether in person or on video. I suggest owning the room, dressed as the CEO, regardless of the potential casual environment; it portrays confidence. I recommend a button-down shirt and dress pants for men or women. It's a timeless style that is my uniform for volunteering as well as client consults. Feel free to make a twist, but please don't get it twisted.

- **Calm your mind and focus:** We all get nervous. Do whatever you have to do to get mentally set. Physically work out at the gym before the interview if that helps, eat a balanced breakfast, arrive on time, and know your professional gifts.

- **Embrace your performer:** Cathy Salit is CEO of Performance of a Lifetime and the author of *Performance Breakthrough: A Radical Approach to Success at Work*. For two decades she has practiced and researched the "Becoming Principle." This is the idea that theatrical performance gives you the transformative power to become who you are in the future. This will help you land a job and make you appear more interesting in the job interview.[3] Read her book for more details on performance for job interviews.

Interviewing is difficult for everyone; we all have jitters. Just remember, you can do this and do it well with a plan and practice.

## BEFORE THE INTERVIEW

After preparing for the content of the interview, it is critical to set up your interviewing environment.

Most hiring companies these days are interviewing through video conferencing. Based on client interactions, there are different levels of familiarity with virtual meeting platforms: Amazon Chime, Cisco WebEx, Google Meet, GoToMeeting, Microsoft Teams, Mikogo, Slack, and Zoom. Depending on whether you are interviewing with an established enterprise company or a startup, it is imperative to practice with their video collaboration application prior to your interview.

A day before the interview, I would sign into the conferencing tool to determine if it is browser-based or if you need to download the application for best performance. This will allow you to understand if your access bandwidth meets the minimum requirements. Clients have turned off video in our discussions, not to hide anything, but to save household shared bandwidth, especially when all children were home schooling last year.

Have you been on a video conference where you were unfamiliar with settings such as sharing files or unmuting participants? It eliminates a worry if you familiarize yourself with a new virtual meeting application. Plus, you typically only have 30 minutes for a 1:1 interview, why waste minutes on troubleshooting?

Once you gain confidence in your video conferencing access, it is time to set the stage for your initial debut with the hiring company. Have you participated in a video conference where some attendees appear to be living in the dark? The way to fix that is to face a sunny window even if your desk is not located accordingly. I have set up temporary placement for calls at my kitchen table or even my couch so I could face the light. If it is dark out, the fix is to put a lamp behind the computer screen to light up your face.

Another item to make your environment more appealing is to unclutter your background. I typically use Microsoft Teams or Zoom for client meetings; both offer options to blur your background. If you do not have that access, make your office more inviting to a viewer by removing distracting items such as exercise equipment or stacks of paper. Or approach this as an opportunity to highlight your strengths and interests; one client displays awards and books that provide a conversation starter with recruiters.

Be on time or a few minutes early since most conferencing applications offer waiting rooms. I am surprised how many clients arrive 5 minutes late to scheduled meetings. To make a favorable impression in an interviewing environment, do not be late. Ever.

## AFTER THE INTERVIEW

Now that your interview is over, there are still impressions to be made. It is time to follow up with a thank you note. In discussions with clients who hire hundreds of team members, they all agree thank you notes are impactful.

One of my collaborators revealed when she was in hiring mode, there were two relatively equal candidates based upon skills and interactions. The candidate selected for the job differentiated himself from the competition by sending a thank you note; it revealed his attention to follow up and detail, which were imperative to the hiring role.

Which brings up the topic of obtaining email addresses from each of the people who interview you. Since you are corresponding with the executive recruiter or HR person, their contact information is available. For additional interviewing panel members, ask for their contact information. A thank you email is a great vehicle to reiterate: what resonates with you about the company culture, mission, or customer solutions, why you want the position, and how you are the perfect candidate for the role.

If for some reason you did not obtain their emails, an alternative is to send a LinkedIn message. While you are at it, ask the interviewers to join your professional network. They have contacts that are beneficial for current and future employment.

What should you say in your thank you note? As part of the interviewing guideline, I created the following template for you to customize.

> Hello <name>, thank you so much for meeting with me today. I enjoyed learning more about your leadership experience at *<company name>* and where you see the company's future.

To follow up on our conversation about *<how to fix an issue or monetize>*, here are my initial ideas:
<idea 1>
<idea 2>

What resonates with me about *<company name>* is you're at the forefront of the technology curve. I would enjoy collaborating with the executive team, building upon your momentum, and growing at hyper-scale.

Best,

<your name>
<city, state>
<telephone | email | your LinkedIn URL>

After preparing your interview content and setting the stage, you are now ready to practice for your close-up.

## EXERCISE: PUT IT INTO PRACTICE

Please go to your worksheet for **Roadmap #4: Master the Interview** and fill out the action plan.

**Action Plan**

1. Stories: Prepare 6 phenomenal stories and write them out with in a 3-part answer format. Remember CAR format: What is the story's context, your actions, and the ultimate result?

a) Your leadership
b) Team building
c) Innovation
d) Problem-solving
e) Biggest mistake
f) Differentiators

2. Record yourself: Tell your 6 remarkable stories out loud in 1-minute and 5-minute versions.

3. Questions: Create 10 questions to ask the recruiter, hiring manager, and panel interviewers. Here is my list to edit.

a) What drew you to the company? What has helped you stay at the company?
b) How has consumer behavior changed since the pandemic?
c) Have you changed your product roadmap during this time? What shifts have you noticed?
d) Could you describe to me your management style and the type of employee that works well with you?
e) Why is this position available? Is this a new role or replacement for another colleague?
f) At the end of the year, how would you know you hired the right person for this position?
g) Whom do you consider your top competitor, and why?
h) What are the most significant opportuni-

ties facing the company/department
right now?

i) Can you tell me about the team I will be
leading?

j) How would you rate the company's
progress on diversity and inclusion? How can
I support the mission?

k) Has the search for this role been moving
quickly, or have you been interviewing for a
while? What have candidates consistently
been missing when you question them?

l) Do you have any hesitations about my qualifications?

## KEY TAKEAWAYS

You are steps away from being camera-ready. You
understand the hiring process is virtual, being
prepared is essential, and practice is key to your
success in a job interview.

In this chapter, about how to **Master the Interview**, you learned about:

- your elevator pitch,
- behavioral questions and technical
  knowledge,
- how to eliminate the jitters, and
- the importance of thank you notes.

In the next chapter, we will focus on the green area
—compensation.

# EXECUTIVE COMPENSATION

If you faced two job offers, how would you arrive at a final decision? You may recall Oliver, the wooden boat builder from the first chapter about **Career Vision**. He faced the dilemma of choosing between two competitive offers. Oliver reached out to me about choosing between a $9.49 billion digital payments company founded in 2009 and a Series B augmented reality (AR) entertainment company with $6 million in funding.

We jumped on the phone to discuss the pros and cons of each; I asked Oliver, "Which one of these are you leaning toward?"

He hesitated before replying, "It is a tough one since they are both profitable. I am torn between being a VP who will be creating cutting-edge products from the ground up versus being an individual contributor and building out a team. The good news is both companies offer a U.S. work visa."

You might recall Oliver was from Australia, so the visa was vital. We switched to focusing on the compensation, and he said, "The digital payments company is offering around the same salary as the other, a $20,000 sign-on bonus and stock, plus I can work from anywhere in the world. The AR company requires that I move from Seattle to Los Angeles, but they are offering over $40,000 for relocation with a 1% bonus."

"Since your former company situation took such a toll on your health, what about the work balance and the people?" I queried.

I heard Oliver's smile over the phone. "The team at the payments company is amazing, and the people are just lovely. My prospective manager has 300 reports with many engineers in my native Australia. The AR company has three very young CxOs with around 100 employees and 40 engineers. I know I will work harder there, but it will feel like less work since I will be building a product."

I realized he could benefit from talking to one of my clients in the AR startup space, so I gave Oliver the contact information.

A week passed, and I texted Oliver on his final answer. You might have guessed it; the wooden boat builder selected the AR company to unleash his building passion. I checked in with Oliver four months later. He is in a state of bliss in his new job, although the cost of living in Los Angeles is a shock to the wallet.

This story proves it is not always just about the compensation for the next role; it is also about your passion. I have experienced this myself, earning high salaries but being just miserable in the position.

In this chapter, about **Executive Compensation**, I will:

- highlight your legal rights related to interview questions,
- outline compensation components, and,
- address the question about your salary requirements.

Whether my clients are tech execs or clients at a not-for-profit, the question always arises, "How do I respond when the recruiter or hiring manager asks me about my current salary or salary expectations?"

It is not straightforward, so I gathered insight from top-notch company negotiators, industry research, and client input.

## LEGAL RIGHTS

I recall an Oracle recruiter phoning me seven years ago regarding an Enterprise Account Director position. Let me preface the discussion context by stating he reached out to me since I was not actively pursuing jobs at the time while at CenturyLink.

Within five minutes, the conversation went to my current salary, and my reply was, "I am not sharing. What is the comp range for this position?"

The recruiter's diversion tactic was saying, "Well, I can't move you forward without knowing your salary."

We did a couple of rounds of this salary point before I politely declined to be in the consideration set. Now granted, we all have received half-baked recruiting requests, but this one from Oracle seemed legitimate. At the time, I did not know the law relating to this question, but I do now.

In Washington state, prospective employers cannot seek your wage or salary history during the interviewing process before making an offer.[1] On the other hand, after the employer negotiates and makes an offer including pay, the employer may confirm your current salary. Some employers require you to sign waivers allowing them to conduct background checks, including your salary, credit history, and job references. Please note that companies in the U.S. are not prohibited from double-checking job applicants' salaries.[2] You will need to check with your current or former company on their policy for disclosing your salary to a prospective employer. This policy varies by company and state.

Also, companies are not legally bound to disclose any information about current or former employees. The majority confirm dates of employment and nothing further because of potential litigation from their current or former employee.

Another interesting fact is that Washington state upholds the open wage discussion, meaning employees can't be prohibited from discussing their wages or the wages of others; wage non-disclosure agreements are not permitted. So, if you live in Washington state, take this as an opportunity to reach out to colleagues where you want to be employed and ask them about the compensation structure.

Although the open wage discussion is true in Washington, that does not mean it is the same for every state. For example, when I lived in Kansas working for Sprint, my boss explicitly told me not to discuss my compensation with others, including the bonus to stay on after the MCI merger. Although the M&A fell apart, I got to keep the sizable bonus, which I recall was worth about 29% of my annual salary.

The good news is that the salary history question, during a job interview, now is banned in a growing number of states and cities.[3] Twenty-eight U.S. states have enacted bans, some city-specific, while others statewide:

- Alabama
- California, Colorado, Connecticut
- Delaware, District of Columbia
- Georgia
- Hawaii
- Illinois
- Kentucky
- Louisiana
- Maine, Maryland, Massachusetts, Mississippi, Missouri
- Nevada, New Jersey, New York, North Carolina
- Ohio, Oregon

- Pennsylvania, Puerto Rico
- Rhode Island
- South Carolina
- Utah
- Vermont, Virginia
- Washington

If a recruiter or hiring manager asks about your current salary, what do you say? I will address that response later in this chapter.

## COMPENSATION COMPONENTS

In a 2020 compensation survey of the top 200 executives at publicly traded companies, Alexander Karp, CEO of Palantir, nailed the #1 spot with $1.1 billion. Palantir went public last year, so Alexander's compensation skyrocketed due to options and stock awards.[4] Only 13 women appeared on the survey list, with Dr. Lisa Su, CEO of Advanced Micro Devices, earning the most of my gender with an annual compensation of $40 million. The monetary amount boggles my mind, but I applaud their achievements.

Most tech executives I work with expect anywhere from $300,000 to $2 million in total compensation. Keep in mind that this is beyond salary, as there are annual and long-term incentives, benefits, perquisites, and severance agreements. According to salary.com's July 2021 Top Division Information Technology Executive report, the average annual salary in Washington state is between $246,802 and $349,641.[5]

What is the best way to know your worth? Conduct a google search with the keyword "salary" for your title, and sources will appear offering free information, including PayScale and GlassDoor. LinkedIn has a feature under the job icon that is available to any subscriber. Type in your desired job title plus city location, and you will see crowd-sourced salary ranges. I believe the LinkedIn numbers are a little low, but it provides a baseline for your consideration.

Compensation is more than just a salary discussion. It would help if you considered all factors, including basics and perks:

- 401K
- Bonuses
- Bringing your pet to work
- Company car or plane usage
- Corporate equity
- Daycare facilities
- Employee assistance
- Guaranteed minimum annual incentive
- Health club membership
- Health insurance
- Life and disability insurance
- Loan to purchase restricted stock, pay taxes or purchase home
- Long-term incentives
- Non-qualified deferred compensation plan
- Office meal delivery
- Parking
- Pension (yes, they still exist, as we learned in a previous chapter)
- Relocation allowance

- Sabbatical
- Salary and wages
- Stock options
- Supplemental executive medical & life insurance
- Telecommuting
- Time off and flexible schedules
- Tuition & certification reimbursement

Boost your confidence and savvy by bringing this intel to the job interview, state what you uncovered, and explain your merits to justify desiring the upper range. Back this up with your years of experience, endorsements, academics, dragon-slaying accomplishments, certifications, and performance appraisals.

## HOW TO RESPOND TO "WHAT IS YOUR SALARY EXPECTATION?"

Since interviewing is not a typical activity for most of us on the other side of the recruiting or hiring manager desk—or video currently—here are a couple of thoughts for your consideration.

Kate Dixon is the Principal and founder of Dixon Consulting, a leadership development and total rewards consultancy specializing in salary-negotiation coaching and compensation solutions. She spent more than 25 years working for and consulting with Nike, Intel, and American Express. She advises not to answer salary history questions. Kate allowed me to review her 2020 book *Pay UP!: Unlocking Insider Secrets of Salary Negotiation*.

I have incorporated her stock answer about salary requirements in my clients' interviewing guideline:

> "Without knowing more about both the role and your pay packages, it's tough to give you a good number here. What is the hiring range for the job so I can be sure we're in the same ballpark?"[6]

## NEGOTIATION & EMPLOYMENT AGREEMENT

One of my book review comments related to how Kate infused a light-hearted perspective on a serious subject with quotes such as "salary negotiation isn't the Hunger Games, and it's definitely not personal."

I am not a lawyer, so I cannot offer legal advice. As a former executive, I can highly recommend getting a legal or compensation expert's opinion regarding an offer or contract. An executive agreement or offer letter is not set in stone, and companies expect negotiations.

Most of my clients ask for increases in base salaries and request sign-on bonuses with stock options or equity. My client Stormy negotiated with a start date nine months out with a multinational company so she could take care of her twins during the pandemic. It was not about money; it was about work-life balance.

When you are negotiating, think about your exit strategy. Whether your exit is your decision or the company's, you should have severance outlined upfront, similar to a marriage prenup. My client

Roger went to work for a startup and was excited about the equity offer; unfortunately, the company did not go IPO, resulting in a liquidation of all assets. With no stipulation in his employment agreement regarding this scenario, all his equity vanished with his job.

It is essential to address upfront any tax liabilities for your compensation package or severance. For stock or equity positions, it is critical to understand the awards and grant documents. There is also the non-compete to consider; I had to sign them at Sprint and CenturyLink. Washington's non-competition law is related to earnings; an employee threshold is $101,390, so a non-compete agreement is considered void and unenforceable under that amount.[7]

## EXERCISE: PUT IT INTO PRACTICE

Please go to your worksheet for **Roadmap #4: Executive Compensation** and fill out the action plan.

**Action Plan**

1. Research your state and city legal rights for answering salary questions and a current or former employer's disclosure policy.
2. Understand a prospective employer's compensation plan by requesting it or reaching out to a colleague who knows the program.
3. Write out your crucial compensation components and non-negotiables.

## KEY TAKEAWAYS

There is a lot to unpack regarding compensation, your legal rights, and what to ask for in an offer.

In this chapter about **Executive Compensation**, you learned about:

- your legal rights related to interview questions,
- compensation components, and,
- addressing your salary requirements.

Congratulations on finishing the fourth roadmap point!

You covered a lot of ground related to your **Job Search**, touching upon:

- executive resumes,
- LinkedIn profiles,
- interviews, and
- executive compensation.

We will pull everything together in the last section, so you hit the ground running with your execution plan.

# Career Roadmap Point #5
## Strategy Implementation

I am a planner in all aspects of my life, highlighted by an affinity for an Excel spreadsheet, whether it is for planning a trip abroad to Greece or creating the book structure from my brain droppings.

I have partnered with more than 200 technology executives. What always captures my attention is their zeal for moving forward to the next job, followed up by a total lack of action. When I analyze my client base, over 50% remain in their current role; it reminds me of signing up for a gym membership in Dallas in my 20s yet never entering the gym. I waved to the gym daily on my way to work at Nortel Networks. The irony is that although financially invested in a health outcome, I quit before engaging in my next steps for a transformation plan. Fast-forward decades later, I set aside 1 hour every day come rain or shine to focus on exercise, whether it is a walk or paddle board session. When you make something a priority, it happens. Do the same in your job search.

At this fifth and last roadmap point, I will focus on your **Strategic Implementation** for your next role. We will apply my clients' success stories so you can:

- create a project plan,
- take a potential sabbatical,
- focus on your job search execution, and,
- make yourself a priority!

# PROJECT PLAN

A weekly 1:1 with my former Kansas City-based boss at CenturyLink altered my life.

With palpable hesitation in his voice, my boss said, "There is good news and bad news. The good news is that the company is re-organizing, and you will continue in your marketing role. The bad news is you have to move from Seattle to Monroe, Louisiana, to keep it."

My head spun. I was not expecting this situation.

The irony was that my career entailed creating project plans for rolling out consumer and enterprise product solutions. Now I needed to apply those same principles to my next career adventure. My rationale was that a project plan would provide a purpose and milestones to check off, highlighting progress. It will do the same for you. With design intent, a written plan provides a confidence booster and structure, when all appears to be going in the wrong direction.

I kicked my plan into gear to stay in Seattle. It evolved into my favorite tool for planning: an Excel spreadsheet. The header columns included contacts to call, jobs to apply for, dates of communication, and status. Since the same company had employed me for 11 years, I did not have an updated resume; therefore, I researched resume writers and found one in Seattle. After an initial phone call, a draft resume, and final edit, I was ready to share my resume with anyone who could endorse and support my efforts; this included former bosses, colleagues, and friends. Next, I went into job application mode with follow-up. Was it easy? No. Frustrating? Yes.

Do you have a project plan for yourself? You should. Otherwise, you may be unprepared if a call comes out of nowhere to move or step down from your current position.

In this chapter about having a **Project Plan**, I will break down how to:

- identify the phases for your job search implementation,
- plan for the next role, and,
- create the actual plan to move forward.

In a U.S. Bureau of Labor Statistics longitudinal study, younger baby boomers held an average of 12.3 jobs from age 18 to age 52. A job is defined as an uninterrupted period of work with a particular employer.[1] My back-of-the-envelope calculation reveals I have had nine jobs during the same age range. Based on these statistics, it stands to reason experts believe a career plan is essential and should be reviewed annually.

In my consulting practice, I have many clients who are certified Professional Management Professionals (PMPs) or Project Managers. They apply predictive, agile, and hybrid approaches for the five phases of the project lifecycle: initiating, planning, executing, monitoring and controlling, and closing. Doesn't it make sense to adopt a similar approach for your job search?

## INITIATING

I conduct a fair amount of research when I take on new projects, and I came across this collegiate advice. Although directed to students enrolled at MIT, this approach applies to wherever you are on your career path.[2]

> "A career plan lists short- and long-term career goals and the actions you can take to achieve them. Career plans can help you make decisions about what classes to take and identify the extracurricular activities, research, and internships that will make you a strong job candidate."

Does this resonate with you? It does with me. I take continuing education courses for executive coaching, writing, book publishing, and foreign languages. Regarding internships, I have mentioned my post-retirement stint as a volunteer career advocate at Dress for Success, which parlayed into my coaching career. I have joined professional associations, such as the WomenTech Network and the International Coaching Federation (ICF) for extracurricular activities.

The following is an 8-step approach from MIT's career planning and professional advising:

- Identify your career options
- Prioritize
- Make comparisons
- Consider other factors
- Make a choice
- Set "SMART" goals: Specific, Measurable, Assignable, Realistic, and Timely
- Create your career action plan
- Meet with a career advisor

At the end of the chapter, I added these eight steps to your workbook exercise activity.

## PLANNING

When Covid hit, I became a virtual career advocate volunteer for Dress for Success in Austin, joining their 6-week 1:1 mentoring program. The *Austin American-Statesman* published an article about this program aimed at career success for women in transition.[3]

"The program is very goal-oriented," says Mia Johns, Dress for Success Austin executive director. She further states that when a woman completes the

Path to Employment program, "she should be ready for a successful jobs search."

They paired me with two women to collaborate on their plans. Lorena was my first mentee who had been unemployed for several years and sought a government job for retirement benefits. She dropped out of the mentoring program after three meetings.

One day out of the blue, I received an email from Lorena with the message, "I started a new job, and I cannot attend the rest of the classes." I congratulated her. While I am still curious about the real story, it is not unusual for people to start and stop suddenly, similar to my gym membership story. I experienced many instances in my volunteer and paid consulting roles when clients dropped out of sessions. My observation is that other factors play into moving forward, whether it is family matters, depression, or a sense of being overwhelmed.

In April 2021, I met my second mentee, the delightful Monica, who was under-employed as a director at a not-for-profit. As a remote employee, she was seeking a better compensation opportunity within the travel industry; this was a tall order, so we needed a plan pronto.

The great news is that Dress for Success Austin developed a project plan as part of the program. Guided by a volunteer manager, we use Google Classroom, a free web service designed for schools to share files between teachers and students. It is where the 6-week syllabus guided Monica and me during the mentoring cohort.

The Dress for Success *"Path to Employment"* plan covers a weekly topic, homework, and checklists for 1-hour video meetups. These are the collaboration topics:

- Goal mapping
- Building your resume and cover letter
- Marketing yourself
- Preparing for your interviews
- Mock interview and job search strategy

These topics should look familiar, as we have touched upon them in previous chapters. Although it took us eight weeks to complete the mentoring cohort due to work and personal factors, Monica successfully completed the program. She arrived with a strong resume foundation but required support for maneuvering from a not-for-profit perspective towards the travel industry with the added twist of working remotely. Now with a plan in hand, she was ready and confident to move forward.

## EXERCISE: PUT IT INTO PRACTICE

Please go to your worksheet for **Roadmap #5: Project Plan** and fill out the action plan.

## Action Plan

1. Identify your career options

   a) Stay at your current employer or look outside the company?
   b) What job titles should you pursue?

2. Prioritize

   a) Which path should you focus on?
   b) Make comparisons

3. What are the pros and cons of the selected paths?

   a) Consider other factors
   b) What are the financial implications?
   c) How does this affect your work-life balance?
   d) What is the stress level for staying versus leaving your current role?

4. Make a choice

   a) Select one path and a job title to move forward

5. Set "SMART" goals

   a) I have heard about SMART goals for years; they have been around since 1981 and were created by Dr. George Doran.[4] In a 2010 YouTube video, Dr. Doran shared that

SMART goals are a tool to get results, not just a checklist.

b) Specific: What are you trying to do? Why are you trying to do this? When will you do what you need to do?

c) Measurable: How will you measure what you are trying to do? Is it by the number of people you will reach out to or interviews you want to obtain?

d) Assignable/Attainable: Do you have the background and contacts to reach your goal? If not, where is the gap, and how do you fix it?

e) Realistic: Can you actually reach the goals you have created? If not, what do you need to undertake to do it?

f) Timely: It is time to reverse engineer by working backward, beginning with your final job search objective, and create the outline for success.

6. Create your career action plan: If you have been completing each of the chapter exercises and the above items, great news, you have a plan! You have gotten to know yourself, explored your occupational options, and evaluated your options.

7. Meet with a career advisor: This could be a mentor, boss, or career coach to review your vision and goals to solicit feedback on your career plan.

## KEY TAKEAWAYS

You may wonder what course of action I took regarding the move to Louisiana. The punchline is that I stayed with CenturyLink for seven more years. I moved from marketing to sales and accrued 18 years of total company service while living in Kansas and Washington state. For many months in advance, I shared with the executive management team that I would retire at the end of the year. It pays to have an executive sponsor; I am indebted to Kim Baker for negotiating an early retirement severance package on my behalf. The extra seven years allowed me to unlock my golden handcuffs, along with a pension and corporate retirement health insurance.

In this chapter about having a **Project Plan**, you learned about:

- identifying the phases for your job search implementation,
- planning for the next role, and
- creating the actual plan to move forward.

In the next chapter, I will delve into a plot twist. How about not working at all?

## POTENTIAL SABBATICAL

Did you ever feel a little envious of a colleague who took off work for six months to cruise the Greek islands, thinking why couldn't that be me? Maybe it is time for you to go on a "Think About."

In 2019 while enjoying delightful seafood pairings with cava for a month on the Costa del Sol in Spain, I penned a blog regarding Fortune 500 companies offering sabbaticals.

The process of writing this book allowed me to reflect on what has transpired in the past two years, ranging from Covid work-at-home policies, my clients' journeys, and the latest research on sabbaticals.

Soulaima Gourani noted in her 2020 Forbes topical sabbatical article:

> "The majority of people who choose sabbatical leave in the United States, England, and

other developed countries are lifelong careerists who are in search of the optimal work-life balance. They have spent years at their jobs without significant breaks other than the one or two weeks of vacation they get each year."[1]

Soulaima further stated that a Facebook VP believed sabbaticals are essential because it allows their most talented employees time to think. I re-coined the term to a "Think About."

In this chapter about taking a **Potential Sabbatical**, I will highlight:

- defining a sabbatical journey,
- looking for a life-work balance, and
- finding companies that offer sabbaticals.

I hear about more and more people taking sabbaticals for work-life balance. It is no longer just for tenured professors and those in the medical field. Some Fortune 500 companies and startups even encourage it.

## WHAT IS A SABBATICAL?

The difference between a sabbatical and a vacation is the time allocation, intention, and proper break from work intensity. A vacation is typically a week or two; a sabbatical is a more extended period of up to a year. It can be the adult version of summer camp with joy, learning, and new adventures. Employers provide this opportunity for employee retention and increased job performance. During a sabbatical, you can recharge and pursue your unique areas of interest. If this stokes your interest, please read on.

My colleagues have gone on sabbatical for various reasons:

- **Decompression**: When you are away from work, your brain can take a career break to return refreshed and energized; it is your time to examine goals and priorities.
- **Education**: How about being able to focus on a master's degree or technical certification, including AWS Certified Architect, Azure, CCNA-Cloud & CCIE, CISSP, PMP, ITL, and Scrum Master without splitting your attention on a full-time job and family responsibilities? You gain a new skill that increases your expertise, job performance, and, ultimately, your paycheck.
- **Life Change**: Although more companies offer parental leave, some new parents want extended family time. On the other end of the life continuum, some colleagues need to take time to care for a parent or family member. I have two clients who took time off during Covid in 2020 to homeschool their children.
- **Exploration**: Many of my colleagues have hobbies they want to explore further without the constraints of working. They are book writers, budding chefs, travel

enthusiasts, and adventurers like me with bucket lists.

## LIFE-WORK BALANCE

Why do we call it a "work-life balance" versus "life-work balance"? Shouldn't we place our personal life first? I think it depends on how much time you spend at work.

Two Harvard professors tracked 27 CEOs of multi-billion-dollar companies; these executives worked on average 62.5 hours weekly, including time while on vacation.[2] If we follow their lead, it means we spend 9.7 hours per weekday at our jobs—commuting, working, problem-solving, agonizing—and only 6.3 hours per day awake in our personal life. This calculation does not yield a work-life balance; I am advocating to switch the ratio toward personal life.

Believe it or not, work-family human resource initiatives help the corporate bottom line. A study of Fortune 500 firms that offered these work-family initiatives drove $60 million in shareholder value.[3] If only everyone embraced personal time off. Have you experienced the boss who made you feel guilty for taking a vacation or leaving early for a family activity? I have.

In the past five years, I have experienced significant changes in my life from early retirement, my mother's death, living abroad for eight months, and starting a consulting practice. Along the way, after soul searching, I have changed my life priorities. I was chatting with my best friend Linda and told her

I approach each day with the following priorities in order of importance: health, personal relationships, and clients.

When I worked in Corporate America, the focus was work, then personal relationships, and, ultimately, my health. Quite a different dynamic. Why on earth was working so important? Because it was my identity, independence, and self-absorbed value —how silly.

How many people from your career or former job are still part of your life? Those bosses you work so hard for in the end do not care when you exit a position. They care, rightly, about their own life. Don't misunderstand me; I keep in touch with a couple of former bosses that care about my well-being. But my advice is to be kind to your significant other and friends since they will be there after that job and are what truly matters in the long run.

## MAKING A CHANGE

Thank you for hanging out with me on this story. Here is what I believe makes for a life-work balance. The secret is scheduling your personal life like your work by simply making time for your health, relationships, passions, and learning.

- **Health**: Make a personal commitment to work out weekly and go to the doctor or dentist. Schedule it on your calendar. Hate exercising? Go golfing or paddle boarding or take up salsa dancing. It is all about being active. It lowers your blood pressure and takes your mind off of business. I call it the reset button. You are switching your focus to a personal need which, in turn, will boost your work performance.

- **Relationships**: Build a network of friends. My friend Linda was a vendor of mine from over 20 years ago. We have not lived in the same city for years, but despite that, we talk on the phone and go on vacation together. Several years ago, we celebrated her husband's birthday in St. Maarten, and it was an incredible experience. What is impressive is that my friend circle continues to evolve at different stages in my life. Fifteen people I socialize with now I only met five years ago. We schedule weekly activities from meals to baseball games, museum outings, and volunteer events.

- **Passions**: Whether it is a sports activity like paddle boarding (mine), daily workouts (mine), or career consulting (mine), I am all in and focused. While I have had many jobs within my varied career path, now I do what I enjoy daily. It took a while to get there, but it was well worth the journey. I now remind myself daily about what is essential.

- **Learning**: I'm the guinea pig for new experiences; Linda and I have attempted three flavors of yoga—hot, aerial, and goat. I'm not making this up. The goat yoga had us in stitches and literally goat poop. My husband came to watch and truly enjoyed hanging out with the friendly goats. We still talk about it, and truthfully, there wasn't an honest attempt at yoga. Who cares? It was plain fun. I signed up for a Spanish class at City University in Seattle to augment my early education and prepare for a 1-month stay in Spain. The class engaged my brain to speak more eloquently and confidently. Plus, I met an interesting new group of people who are at least 15 years younger than me and bring in different perspectives.

- **Giving Back:** You will gain more than you can ever give by volunteering. Over dinner, I asked my husband how he achieved life-work balance, and he said it was by volunteering plus being the captain of his tennis league. He volunteered for Junior Achievement while working as an engineering executive in Atlanta; giving back to the community for what he had received growing up in Brooklyn. For those of you unfamiliar, Junior Achievement is the world's largest organization dedicated to educating students in grades K-12 about entrepreneurship, work readiness, and financial literacy through experiential, hands-on programs.

## COMPANIES OFFERING SABBATICALS

*Fortune Magazine*, ForceBrands, Glassdoor, and Built In have compiled lists of hiring companies offering sabbaticals after 5-10 years of service, from four weeks up to 12 months in the case of Starbucks.[4] Are there any surprises here in this list for you?

- AARP, Adobe, Alert Media, Alta Planning + Design, Aptitive, Ascent, AuthO, Autodesk, Away
- Bain & Company, Betterment, Biogen, Blue Moon Digital, BrewDog
- Car Gurus, Casper, Cedar, Centro, Charles Schwab, Checkr, Chicago Public Schools, ChowNow, Cisco Meraki, CLEAR, Clif Bar, Club Automation, Cloudflare, Code3, Code Climate, Coder, Cognite, Cohesion, Coinbase, Course Hero
- Deloitte, Doximity, Drift
- eBay, Enigma, Enova, Ensono, Envoy Global, Epic, EzCater
- Genentech, Grammarly, Greenhouse Software
- Harry's, Havenly, Headway, HIMSS, HomeLight
- Immersive Labs, InfluxData, Intel, Invitae
- Jelly Vision, Justworks
- Kinship, Kyruus
- Logic20/20
- Matillion, Maven Clinic, Maxwell, Melio, Mentor Collective, Modern Times, Modernize Home Services, MongoDB, mParticle, Morningstar
- New Belgium, Newsela
- oak9, OCC, OJO Labs, Onna, One Medical
- Pangea Money Transfer, PayPal, Peak6, Perkins Coie, PerkSpot, PHYTEC America, Pitchbook, PopSockets LLC, Prefect, Purchasing Platform
- Real Chemistry, Redgate Software, REI,

Rent the Runway, Rev.com, Reverb, RightHand Robotics, Rokt

- Scaled Agile, Sift, Simply Business, Skillshare, Soofa, Spins LLC, Stack Overflow, Starbucks, Surefront
- Tamr, Teachers Pay Teachers, theSkimm, Thoughtworks, Toast, ThrivePass, TrueAccord, Trupanion
- Uber
- Vistaprint, Vivid Seats
- Webflow, Whole Foods Market
- Yieldstreet, Yotpo, Your Super
- Zello, Zen Planner

## SABBATICALS ON YOUR DIME

In the past 12 months, I have worked with three clients who decided to stop working entirely because they were emotionally exhausted. One common theme was that they had all worked at a startup along the way.

You might recall Oliver, the wooden boat builder, from chapter one on **Career Vision**. While I was collaborating on job opportunities with the 45-year-old, a health scare landed him in the hospital and required heart monitoring. This incident made him question staying at his current company since his role became a stress inducer and a cultural mismatch. His preference was to return to his builder persona at a startup helping people and making the world a better place. He upped and quit, taking a personal sabbatical. Oliver had no job prospects along with the extra burden of a visa requirement to stay in the U.S. since he hailed from Australia. What did he do? Oliver went on a 6-month "Think About," including pursuing life on the beach in Maui for a month.

Next, Oliver went to a small town in Mexico to hang out with friends for introspection. He came back to Seattle recharged. The best news was that the career break not only improved his health, but he now had new career prospects. He sent me a text to discuss two job offers: a California-based augmented reality (AR) startup and a 6-year-old FinTech company where he could live anywhere on the globe. Ultimately, he chose the AR startup.

In January, I received an email from Merry. As it turns out, she was best friends with a current client I had been partnering with on a potential exit from Microsoft. Merry was a former Microsoft Chief of Staff and serial intrapreneur on a 1.5-year sabbatical. After leaving her COO startup role and consulting side hustle, she decided to re-enter the corporate world. After our collaboration to position her for the next role, we touched base several times. Family matters interceded with her job search. She pinged me this week to let me know she's now back at Microsoft with an equitable compensation package.

Cesar had 18 years' career experience at six Fortune 500 companies and was a VP of product strategy at a $33MM IT platform startup. He had high endorsements for cloud computing and enterprise software. His global career spanned the cities of Boston, D.C., London, San Francisco, and Seattle. He left a company after four years and was on a personal sabbatical when we met. For his next role, Cesar wanted to lead the product or service development for a mission-oriented organization. The scope would be leading global change in an industry with mission orientation and a clear-cut direction of the purpose of the business, e.g., reinvent transportation for the 21$^{st}$ century like Uber.

After our collaboration, I checked in on him six months later. Cesar continues to work part-time at the startup he founded several years ago. He moved from Seattle and now lives in the wine country of Napa Valley, California.

## MY SABBATICAL

When I worked for corporations, even when I was on vacation, I was still conducting business, since I had a monthly sales quota.

A year into my consulting practice, I took a month off. I put my clients and volunteer commitments on hold. Blogging was allowed since I created the company's rules. So, what did my husband Pat and I decide to do? We went to Málaga, Spain, for a month as part of our 10-year travel adventure bucket list.

How did I select this place? I was enchanted by our month's stay in Sitges outside of Barcelona a couple of years previous, so I looked at the map and found the biggest-font city on Google maps along the East coast in Spain. That is how the Montaninos figure it out—by the font size.

Pat and I spend on average 60 days outside the U.S. In 2020 we went to Argentina, Uruguay, and Mexico. We establish our daily routines in global venues.

What all these sabbatical stories I have shared with you have in common is a time for personal reflection; it is embracing a life-work balance.

## EXERCISE: PUT IT INTO PRACTICE

Please go to your worksheet for **Roadmap #5: Potential Sabbatical** and fill out the action plan.

**Action Plan**

If I had a career do-over, I would have focused more on my personal life. Here is an opportunity for you to reflect on life-work balance.

1. Life-Work Balance Assessment

   a) Daily, how much time do you focus on work?
   b) Daily, how much time do you spend awake focused on your personal life?
   c) Now, to face reality, journal for one week how many hours you spend working daily. Do they match what you guessed?

2. Sabbatical

   a) If you were to take a 6-month sabbatical, what would you do with your time?
   b) Of the top five companies in your consideration set, do they offer sabbaticals? Check

out their website benefits page. Write down the ones that offer a sabbatical; it's a point to mention during your interview or cover letter as a hook.

## KEY TAKEAWAYS

The good news is that you can take time for extended periods from work, come back refreshed, and move on to your next career adventure. If you are at a crossroads, now is the time to either allow yourself a "Think About," or find a company that will provide that option in the future.

In this chapter about taking a **Potential Sabbatical**, you learned about:

- defining a sabbatical journey,
- looking for a life-work balance, and
- finding companies that offer sabbaticals.

In the next chapter, we will put all that you have learned in this book into action.

## JOB SEARCH EXECUTION

Ted was an IT Director at a government consultancy. When we first spoke on the phone, he told me that after submitting 50 resumes, there had been zero response. Wow! He felt that there was a missing element but could not quite pinpoint the issue. Ted's three former employers had hired him due to his 11 years of Microsoft experience as a software test lead, so the recruiters' radio silence struck a blow to his psyche. Clearly, the bloom was off the rose. Fifteen years had transpired since he had worked at Microsoft.

Now Ted wanted to move back to Microsoft as a QA Director within the gaming business unit. Why? As a car fanatic, he thoroughly enjoyed working on the Microsoft Studio X team for the Forza Motorsport project.

I asked Ted a couple of questions related to networking. "Have you reached out to anyone at Microsoft from your past? Do you know who the

hiring manager might be for this particular job you
are interested in?"

The response was, "Not really. I don't really have
many contacts over there since it's been a while."

I conducted LinkedIn research targeting a
Microsoft General Manager who handled gaming
and searched for employees with titles that might be
a manager or peer. I handed Ted a list of three
suspects and wrote a 5-sentence customized email
for him to distribute.

Ted sent a LinkedIn Inmail, and the response from
one person was immediate, stating he was not the
hiring manager but would forward on the resume.
That is called networking. You can and should do it
to increase your odds of connecting with the appro-
priate decision-maker, influencer, or support person
for your next role.

Last I checked, Ted has not changed jobs yet.

Another idea I employ is following potential hiring
managers on LinkedIn, Instagram, or Twitter. The
former will provide information about what is essential to them in business, while the latter two offer
more of a personal perspective given away in their
bio or tweets.

I recently used these sources for an executive
director of cloud enablement at a Fortune 50. Laxmi
wanted to work for a Corporate VP of Cross-
Industry Solutions at another company. I spent a
couple of hours profiling Laxmi's targeted next boss
and then created a personalized email to him. Laxmi
was enamored with the Corporate VP's accomplish-

ments, including an Accenture-endorsed book. The book received a 4.5 rating on Amazon with stunning reviews by Satya Nadella, Andy Jassy, Michael Dell, and Klaus Schwab, founder and executive chairman of the World Economic Forum.

How did Laxmi know where to send the email? I introduced her to a Microsoft client who provided Laxmi the VP's work email address. Did she hear back yet? No, so I told her to reach out with a connection request on LinkedIn. Persistence is critical, and it is an admirable quality.

By now, you have created your career vision and completed the end-of-chapter exercises. You have planned where you want to arrive and what you need to achieve for your subsequent role. Now it's time to put your hard work into action. The execution phase is traditionally the longest part of your job search and the most demanding.

To simplify your endeavor, I created a career plan execution checklist with goals and completion dates. Before we go there, it's time to focus on your professional network.

In this chapter, focus on your **Job Search Execution** by:

- understanding the importance of networking,
- consolidating your career plan, and
- implementing your project based upon goal and completion dates.

## PROFESSIONAL NETWORKING STATISTICS

In trying to determine the latest job-hunting statistics, I have observed that most career experts source information from a 2011 article that said 70% of jobs are never published.[1] I imagine over the course of the last decade job posting sites, such as LinkedIn, ExecThread, and Indeed have reduced that percentage, but even if 50% of jobs are not posted, it is something you should consider.

This secret job phenomenon leads me to another outdated statistic that 85% of jobs are filled through networking.[2] Once again, even if the percentage dropped by half, it points to the fact that you need to address your networking game. Networking is one of the biggest challenges for most clients since their careers typically were a series of jobs handed to them by someone they knew.

If your networking game is not up to par, it's time to embrace the challenge. Over 90% of the jobs I received in my career were due to personal relationships versus sending a blind email to an online posting. The latter does work, but you increase your chances for an interview by reaching out to colleagues or new acquaintances at your target dream company.

Offer to buy lunch or grab a coffee or tea to learn more about the corporate culture. Granted, it is uncomfortable, but what is a new career worth to you?

When I began volunteering at Dress for Success and subsequently started my executive career consultancy, I enhanced my existing career network with a new set of people. These physical and virtual connections are new clients, volunteer associates, admirable coaches, and book authors, leading to my global network expansion across the Americas, Europe, and the Middle East.

## EXERCISE: PUT IT INTO PRACTICE

Please go to your worksheet for **Roadmap #5: Job Search Execution** and fill out your career action plan.

**Career Plan + Execution Steps**

1. **Career vision**:

I am a _____

_____

who wants to be _____

_____

*Refer back to roadmap #1 Career Path/Career Vision exercise.*

2. **Mission statement**: Describe what you do, for who, and how.

_____

_____

_____

*Refer back to roadmap #1 Career Path/Indecision exercise.*

3. **Core values**: List the top 5 beliefs and behaviors to achieve your vision and mission.

_____

_____

_____

_____

_____

*Refer back to roadmap #1 Career Path/Indecision exercise.*

4. **Career Path**: Select 1 path and a job title to move forward.

_____

_____

*Refer back to roadmap #1 Career Path/Indecision exercise*

5. **Skills Mapping**: Find 3 job postings based upon your career path.
a)   List the soft skills that appear a minimum of 2 times across the postings.

_____

_____

_____

b)   List the hard skills that appear a minimum of 2 times across the postings.

_____

_____

_____

*Refer back to roadmap #2 C-Suite Advice/Think Like a CEO.*

6. **Your Superpowers**: Identify your top 3 leadership skills + top 3 domain skills.

_____
_____
_____
_____
_____
_____

*Refer back to roadmap #3 Personal Brand/What is Your Superpower?*

7. **Elevator Pitch**: Limit it to 4-5 sentences and time it for being under 1 minute.

_____
_____
_____
_____
_____
_____

*Refer back to roadmap #3 Personal Brand/Elevator Pitch.*

8. **Execution Plan**
*Refer back to roadmap #4 Job Search Tools.*

a)  Set aside 1 hour per day for job search
*Goal date _____ Completion date _____*

b)  Revise resume
*Goal date _____ Completion date _____*

c)  Update LinkedIn profile
*Goal date _____ Completion date _____*

d)  Clean up your social media

*Goal date* _____ *Completion date* _____

e)  Start posting and commenting on LinkedIn
*Goal date* _____ *Completion date* _____

f)  Cover letter created to be customized by role
*Goal date* _____ *Completion date* _____

g)  Rehearse 6 phenomenal interviewing stories
*Goal date* _____ *Completion date* _____

h)  Meet with your mentor or coach
*Goal date* _____ *Completion date* _____

i)  Sign up for a professional association
*Goal date* _____ *Completion date* _____

j)  Join a volunteer board
*Goal date* _____ *Completion date* _____

k)  Create list of top 5 companies in consideration
*Goal date* _____ *Completion date* _____

l)  Compile list of 2 people within each company
for networking
*Goal date* _____ *Completion date* _____

m) Contact networking list for 15-minute discussion
regarding culture and roles you are interested in
applying for
*Goal date* _____ *Completion date* _____

n)  Identify job postings 1 day per week
*Goal date* _____ *Completion date* _____

o)   Apply for 1-2 jobs per week
*Goal date* _____ *Completion date* _____

p)   Prepare for the interview
*Goal date* _____ *Completion date* _____

q)   Send thank you emails post interviews
*Goal date* _____ *Completion date* _____

r)   Negotiate the offer
*Goal date* _____ *Completion date* _____

s)   Accept the job, congratulations!

## KEY TAKEAWAYS

Does everyone accept my invitation to meet or connect when I reached out via email, phone call, or LinkedIn? No, but rejection is part of the journey, so acknowledge that and move on. Surprisingly, sometimes people follow up with me months later. The critical thing to remember is that you will need to network and campaign for yourself for your execution plan to work. Since job hunting is a rare event, you are now up to date on what job search tricks will augment your chances of becoming an online click magnet for tech executive recruiters.

In this chapter, for your **Job Search Execution**, you learned about:

- gained an understanding of the importance of networking,
- consolidated your career plan, and
- implemented your plan based upon goal and completion dates.

In the next chapter, we will discuss the importance of the prioritization of someone you know well. Oh, that would be you!

# MAKING YOURSELF A PRIORITY

Here's the reality, most of my clients drag their feet. I am astounded at the number of clients interested in advancing their career journeys and then procrastinating. My minimum condition for client engagements is that we can start working within one week. That is the virtual handshake, but it's not the reality.

Take, for example, William, a CEO of a forecasting and IT company acquired by Bain for $300 million. We connected on the phone back in March 2021, and he paid me in full for my consulting. I have followed up six times to meet with him, and here I am five months later without any word from William. He left his former company and is currently unemployed, enjoying a summer sabbatical based on his LinkedIn profile. I imagine he has extra time on his hands, but his priority is not finding employment with my support. After 21 years of focusing on his career, I think it is admirable for William to take time off.

Then there is Ashok, a Microsoft GM, who hired me in July 2019 with an urgent need to create an executive resume within five days. Yet, the entire personal branding project, including the initial resume request, was not completed until October. The reality was the 5-day resume request was a smokescreen deadline. Four months passed while Ashok traveled on business and vacationed for a month in India. My clients' and my motivations are somewhat different. In July, the Microsoft GM needed the resume for the specific executive recruiter request, while I wanted to complete the job to earn compensation. In January 2020, Ashok left his 17-year Microsoft career to become a Senior VP at a Fortune 500 mass media company. I applaud Ashok for achieving his goal of becoming a VP of a media business to deliver video at scale by leveraging AI and data assets.

Amaira was dramatically different from William and Ashok. From the start, she had a prioritized focus for her next role. In turn, we developed her branding, resume, cover letter, and LinkedIn profile and fine-tuned her interviewing skills within two weeks. Within less than a month, she was interviewing for director roles at Microsoft and AWS. She received two offers, which exhibits that being highly motivated pays off.

My clients fall into four major categories when it comes to prioritization.

- **The Out-of-Towner**: 15% of clients travel for work or vacation, and they do not utilize that time to complete our consulting collaboration. For example, in Ashok's case, the questionnaire remained unanswered, and his resume edits were put on hold even though he was on a 16-hour flight from the U.S. to India.

- **The Work Perpetrator**: 25% of clients put their current workload as a higher priority than looking for a job. The irony is that they dislike what they are doing but focus more on that than a job search implementation strategy.
- **The Ghost**: 25% of clients contact me, agree to move forward, and then I never hear from them again. In some cases, such as William's, they even prepay; I call it procrastination money. Hey, I will take it to pay my business operating expenses.
- **The Action Hero**: 35% of clients meet with me, and we complete their initial project within 10 business days. They prove that actions speak louder than words; the majority, like Amaira, land jobs within 1-4 months.

In this chapter, for **Making Yourself a Priority**, I will:

- discuss what works well for my client's success,
- highlight motivation research, and
- provide ideas to become the Action Hero.

According to Dr. Bryan Robinson, "procrastination is an unconscious way your mind tries to take away the anxiety of 'Can I do it perfectly?' so postponing seems to bring relief in the short term while undermining your career in the long run. If you avoid the looming project, you temporarily avoid the judgment and self-doubt."[1]

I will feature a subset of Dr. Robinson's tips to conquer procrastination in your final book exercise.

In the past year, I have read blogs and watched videos mentioning hitting the start button when pursuing new avenues. It sounds simple, yet it is challenging for some to begin their executive career, face a mid-life assessment, or plan to retire within five years. It prompted me to research how to prioritize yourself if you do not define yourself as the Action Hero.

## CAREER MOTIVATION

Although there is limited academic research regarding job search behavior, I found one in the *Journal of Applied Psychology* related to personality-motivational analysis. It identified six variables for job search success: personality traits, generalized expectations, self-evaluations, motives, social context, and biographical variables.

> "Job search is more strongly related to psychological variables encompassed by the broader construct of positive affectivity (e.g., extroversion, conscientiousness, self-esteem, job search efficacy) than to variables encompassed by the broad construct of negative

affectivity (e.g., neuroticism, agreeableness)."[2]

In a nutshell, a positive job search outcome relates to your effort, mindset, and motivations.

I am highly self-motivated when it comes to certain things, are you? Gosh, I am motivated to monitor my health, pursue joy, help others, maintain friendships, and complete my global travel bucket list. Cleaning, not so much. Sometimes the living room rug goes two weeks without vacuuming. Why? My former motivation related to self-image was not warranted when Covid restricted visitors; remnants of my husband's pistachio shells appear under the couch. Pat explained to me that he does not look down, so it does not bother him—proving sometimes motivation wanes based upon circumstances including age, focus, and lack of guests.

According to Dr. Kou Murayama, a professor at the Hector Research Institute of Education Sciences and Psychology at Tübingen University, motivation science is an emerging research area.[3] The shocker to me is the nascent aspect of this field of research. It turns out while motivation is related to everything we think or do, there is academic segregation for motivation theories in a psychology focus, whether educational, social, organizational, or cognitive neuroscience. If you collapse them under one umbrella, that's called motivation science. I am pretty familiar with motivation science since my initial career focused on it for corporate brand positioning.

Decades ago, I was an adjunct professor teaching consumer behavior to undergraduate and graduate students at The University of Texas at Dallas.

The syllabus focused on what human values drive and motivate consumers to purchase something or take action, such as voting. It is related to Maslow's 5-tier hierarchy of human needs in motivational theory: physiological (food and water), safety (employment), love and belonging (family), self-esteem (achievement), and self-actualization (meaning and inner potential).[4]

My teaching examples related to corporate clients who wanted to figure out why consumers purchased cars, ate salty snacks, selected a political candidate, or joined the army.

In 1:1 interviews with young adults between the ages of 18 and 21, I was intrigued by what motivated them to enlist in the military. Our consumer behavior research highlighted positive reinforcements, as well as the avoidance of negative consequences. For some, the military was a means of escaping a bad situation at home or simply growing up by learning discipline, leadership principles, and teamwork. For others, it was a way to pay for a college education or continue a family tradition of service for honor and recognition.

In psychology, there are four major types of motivation related to a person's behavior and pursuit of goals.[5]

- **Extrinsic**: Refers to behavior driven by external rewards such as money, fame,

grades, and praise. This type
of motivation arises from outside the
individual.

- **Intrinsic**: Opposed to
extrinsic motivation, intrinsic originates
inside of the individual. You participate in
an activity like sports or reading for its own
sake versus external reward.

- **Introjected**: Generated by guilt, worry, or
shame. This is somewhat external. You
enact a behavior not because you want to
but fear of obligation to a parent, friend, or
manager.

- **Identified**: You have recognized the
importance of a behavior and have accepted
it in achieving a goal; this is somewhat
internal. An identified motivation does not
mean you have to find enjoyment in taking
action. Recall the moments when you
genuinely believe exercise is worth doing
because it's right for you, and the benefits
are valuable. I mentioned previously
purchasing a gym membership and waving
every time I drove down the street but
failed to drop in.

What does all this mean? People want to advance in
their careers but are challenged by executing the
steps based upon different motivations. In my opinion, universities and companies do not train us
adequately for success in this endeavor. I had a CIO
client mention there is a vast void for a job search
since you can't discuss it with anyone at your current

company. Plus, it is not something you conduct on an annual basis.

It's time for you to become the Action Hero. Do not wait until you need a job; start today. Regardless of the time of the year, please invest in yourself. Better yet, make it a quarterly initiative to honor your career advancement goals.

## EXERCISE: PUT IT INTO PRACTICE

Please go to your worksheet for **Roadmap #5: Making Yourself a Priority** and fill out your career action plan.

**Action Plan**

1. Hold Yourself Accountable: When I put my intentions out in the Universe, my pride kicks in to achieve it. Based on my husband's encouragement, I blogged last year about writing a book. Initially, Pat would ask me daily if I had started writing. Besides some high-level research, I hadn't fully committed. It changed when I began my new year in earnest with a 2021 publishing deadline. You are reading the result.

2. Identify an Incentive: When I was in sales, there was an annual incentive to go on the company's Circle of Excellence trip in an exotic locale for top quota achieving producers. The year I left CenturyLink, I reached my sales quota pinnacle, so my husband joined me on a trip to stay at The

Breakers in Palm Beach, Florida, for several days. We have fond memories of that trip including sailing, cooking classes at Sur Le Table, and being treated in a top-notch fashion. Take a moment to identify an incentive to spur you on your job search, whether that's a trip with your family, home renovation, funding your child's education, or buying that EV-charging car.

3. Break Things Down: If you completed the previous chapter's **Job Search Execution** exercise, you have compiled a list of approximately 18 items to achieve success. Use this as your checklist for moving forward in your job search.

4. Challenge Yourself: You completed your SMART goals, so refer to it weekly to challenge yourself to meet your timelines. For the month of August, I challenged myself to edit a book chapter within two days. I achieved my goal of editing 20 chapters by documenting results on my word tracker Excel spreadsheet. It provided peace of mind and a sense of accomplishment for meeting my goals.

Congratulations on completing the 5-point roadmap!

- **Career Path**: develop your career vision, confront indecision, evaluate corporate versus startups roles, and consider remote positions
- **C-Suite Advice**: think like a CEO, benefit from mentor and coach collaborations,

invest in your continuing education, and
join boards for networking opportunities
and social impact
- **Personal Brand**: harness your superpower,
  identify your top skills, create an elevator
  pitch, embrace social media, and address
  diversity and inclusion
- **Job Search Tools**: investigate the best
  practices for executive resumes, LinkedIn
  profiles, interviews, and executive
  compensation
- **Strategy Implementation**: create a
  project plan, take a potential sabbatical,
  focus on job search execution, and, most
  importantly, make yourself a priority!

You have taken steps to focus on your career vision,
job search strategy, and tactics for your next job. I
hope you learned a trick or two in becoming an
online click magnet for executive recruiters as a
technology executive or aspiring one. If you have
read the chapters and completed the exercises,
you're on your way to becoming a tech provocateur,
landing your next significant role, and putting on a
set of golden handcuffs, if that's your goal.

When you succeed as the Action Hero, please drop
me a line; I am a champion for a happy ending.

I want to thank you very much for purchasing and
reading this book.

# BIBLIOGRAPHY

"10 Tips for Developing A Strong Personal Brand."
*Forbes*. July 21, 2018.
https://www.forbes.com/sites/forbesagencycouncil/
2018/07/21/10-tips-for-developing-a-strong-personal-
brand/?sh=13dd84a9b705.

"16 Personalities." Accessed July 17, 2021.
https://www.16personalities.com/free-personality-
test.

"71% of Hiring Decision-Makers Agree Social Media
is Effective for Screening Applicants." Express
Employment Professionals. October 13, 2020.
https://www.expresspros.com/Newsroom/America-
Employed/71-of-Hiring-Decision-Makers-Agree-
Social-Media-is-Effective-for-Screening-
Applicants.aspx.

"2018 Membership Marketing Benchmarking Report." Marketing General Incorporated. 2018. https://nacmnet.org/wp-content/uploads/The-2018-Membership-Marketing-Benchmarking-Report-Highlighted.pdf.

"2020 ICF Global Coaching Study Executive Summary." International Coaching Federation. September 2020. https://coachingfederation.org/app/uploads/2020/09/FINAL_ICF_GCS2020_ExecutiveSummary.pdf.

"50/50 Women on Boards Gender Diversity Directory™." 50/50 Women on Boards. Accessed August 1, 2021. https://5050wob.com/directory/.

"About IEEE." IEEE. Accessed August 1, 2021. https://www.ieee.org/about/index.html.

"About Us." LinkedIn.com. Accessed August 31, 2021. https://news.linkedin.com/about-us#Statistics.

Adelson, Robert A., Esq. "Executive Service on Corporate Board of Directors – Benefits, Liabilities and Compensation." *CEOWorld Magazine*. February 21, 2019. https://ceoworld.biz/2019/02/21/executive-service-on-corporate-boards-of-directors-benefits-liabilities-and-compensation/.

Adler, Lou. "New Survey Reveals 85% of All Jobs are Filled Via Networking." LinkedIn. February 28, 2016.
https://www.linkedin.com/pulse/new-survey-reveals-85-all-jobs-filled-via-networking-lou-adler/.

"Annual Estimates of the Resident Population for Selected Age Groups by Sex for the United States: April 1, 2010, to July 1, 2019." U.S. Census Bureau. June 25, 2020.
https://www2.census.gov/programs-surveys/popest/tables/2010-2019/national/asrh/nc-est2019-agesex.xlsx.

Baumeister, Roy F. and John Tierney. *Willpower: Rediscovering the Greatest Human Strength*. New York: Penguin Press, 2011.

Bennett, Karen. "13 Surprising Companies Who Still Give Out Pensions." Cheatsheet.com. May 5, 2018.
https://www.cheatsheet.com/money-career/surprising-companies-give-out-pensions.html/.

"Best Global Brands 2020." Interbrand. Accessed August 29, 2021.
https://www.interbrand.com/best-brands/.

"Best Executive MBA Programs 2021." College Consensus. September 9, 2020.
https://www.collegeconsensus.com/rankings/best-emba-programs/.

Botelho, Elena Lytkina, Kim Rosenkoetter Powell, Stephan Kincaid, and Dina Wang. "What Sets

Successful CEOs Apart," *Harvard Business Review*.
May-June 2017.
https://hbr.org/2017/05/what-sets-successful-ceos-
apart.

Bracetti, Alex. "Gallery: Tech CEOs With Their
Mentors." Complex.com. July 23, 2012.
https://www.complex.com/pop-culture/2012/07/
gallery-tech-ceos-with-their-mentors/.

Brigham, Tess. "I've been a 'millennial therapist' for
more than 5 years—and this is their No. 1
complaint." CNBC make it. Updated July 3, 2019.
https://www.cnbc.com/2019/07/02/a-millennial-
therapist-brings-up-the-biggest-complaint-they-
bring-up-in-therapy.html.

Callahan, Sean. "Picture Perfect: Make A Great First
Impression with Your LinkedIn Profile Photo."
*LinkedIn Sales Blog* (blog). December 28, 2018.
https://www.linkedin.com/business/sales/blog/b2b-
sales/picture-perfect--make-a-great-first-impression-
with-your-linkedi.

Coutu, Diane and Carol Kauffman. "What Can
Coaches Do For You?" *Harvard Business Review*. Last
modified January 2009.
https://hbr.org/2009/01/what-can-coaches-
do-for-you.

Cerdeira, Nicolas and Kyril Kotashev. "Startup
Failure Rate: Ultimate Report + Infographic [2021]."
*Failory* (blog). Accessed July 17, 2021.
https://www.failory.com/blog/startup-failure-rate.

Dixon, Kate. Pay UP!: Unlocking Insider Secrets of Salary Negotiation. Portland, OR: Oceanside Press, 2020.

Doran, George T. "There's a S.M.A.R.T way to write management's goals and objectives." *Management Review* 70.11 (Nov. 1981): 35.

"Elevator Pitch." Wikipedia. Accessed August 3, 2021. https://en.wikipedia.org/wiki/Elevator_pitch.

"Encyclopædia Britannica." Wikipedia. Accessed August 29, 2021. https://en.wikipedia.org/wiki/Encyclopædia_Britannica

"Equal Pay & Opportunities Act." Washington State Department of Labor & Industrives. Accessed August 16, 2021. https://lni.wa.gov/workers-rights/wages/equal-pay-opportunities-act/.

"Four Motivations." Changing Minds. Accessed August 28, 2021. http://changingminds.org/explanations/motivation/four_motivations.htm.

"Gartner HR Survey Shows 86% of Organizations Are Conducting Virtual Interviews to Hire Candidates During Coronavirus Pandemic." Gartner. April 30, 2020. https://www.gartner.com/en/newsroom/press-releases/2020-04-30-gartner-hr-survey-shows-86--of-organizations-are-cond.

Glassdoor Team. "14 Companies Offering Sabbaticals & Hiring Now," *Glassdoor* (blog), November 9, 2018,
https://www.glassdoor.com/blog/42136-2/.

"Global social networks ranked by numbers of user 2021." Statista. August 2, 2021.
https://www.statista.com/statistics/272014/global-social-networks-ranked-by-number-of-users/.

Gourani, Soulaima. "Why Employers Should Embrace Sabbatical Leave Programs." *Forbes*. January 24, 2020.
https://www.forbes.com/sites/soulaimagourani/2020/01/24/why-employers-should-embrace-sabbatical-leave-programs/?sh=7e12b8847c05.

"Handwriting vs. Typing: How to Choose the Best Method to Take Notes." Effectiviology.com. Accessed July 25, 2021.
https://effectiviology.com/handwriting-vs-typing-how-to-take-notes/#Note-taking_and_your_memory.

Horrigan, John B. "Lifelong Learning and Technology." Pew Research Center. March 22, 2016.
https://www.pewresearch.org/internet/2016/03/22/lifelong-learning-and-technology/.

"Is It Legal for a Prospective Employer to Verify Your Current Salary?" The Law Dictionary. Accessed August 17, 2021. https://thelawdictionary.org/article/is-it-illegal-for-a-prospective-employer-to-verify-your-current-salary/.

Kaufman, Wendy. "A Successful Job Search: It's All About Networking." NPR. February 3, 2011. https://www.npr.org/2011/02/08/133474431/a-successful-job-search-its-all-about-networking.

Kanfer, Ruth & Wanberg, Connie & Kantrowitz, Tracy. "Job search and employment: A personality-motivational analysis and meta-analytic review." *Journal of Applied Psychology* 86 (2001): 837-855.

Kowarski, Ilana. "What an Executive MBA Is and Reasons to Get One." *U.S. News & World Report*. November 14, 2019. https://www.usnews.com/education/best-graduate-schools/top-business-schools/articles/what-an-executive-mba-is-and-how-it-compares-to-a-full-time-mba.

Ladders Contributor. "Do cover letters still matter? Here's what data shows." The Ladders. June 19, 2019. https://www.theladders.com/career-advice/do-cover-letters-still-matter-heres-what-data-shows.

Laker, Ben, Will Godley, Selin Krudet, and Rita Trehan. "4 Tips to Nail a Virtual Job Interview." *Harvard Business Review*. March 9, 2021. https://hbr.org/2021/03/4-tips-to-nail-a-virtual-job-interview.

Lerner, Diane. "Board of Directors Compensation: Past, Present, and Future." Harvard Law School Forum on Corporate Governance. March 14, 2017. https://corpgov.law.harvard.edu/2017/03/14/board-of-directors-compensation-past-present-and-future/.

"Lesbian, Gay, Bisexual, and Transgender Workplace Issues (Quick Take)." Catalyst Research. June 1, 2021.
https://www.catalyst.org/research/lesbian-gay-bisexual-and-transgender-workplace-issues/.

Lipnic, Victoria A. "The State of Age Discrimination and Older Workers in the U.S. 50 Years After the Age Discrimination in Employment Act (ADEA)." U.S. Equal Employment Opportunity Commission. June 2018.
https://www.eeoc.gov/reports/state-age-discrimination-and-older-workers-us-50-years-after-age-discrimination-employment.

MacKay, Jory. "Productivity in 2017: What we learned from analyzing 225 million hours of work time." *RescueTime* (blog). January 4, 2018.
https://rescuetime.wpengine.com/225-million-hours-productivity/.

"Make a Career Plan." MIT Career Advising & Professional Development. Accessed August 18, 2011.
https://capd.mit.edu/resources/make-a-career-plan/.

Marcec, Dan. "Equilar | New York Times 200 Highest-Paid CEOs." Equilar. June 11, 2021.
https://www.equilar.com/reports/82-equilar-new-york-times-top-200-highest-paid-ceos-2021.

Maslow, A.H. "A Theory of Human Motivation." *Psychological Review*, 50 (1943): 370-396.

http://www.researchhistory.org/2012/06/16/maslows-hierarchy-of-needs/.

McNamara, Carter. "Overview of Roles & Responsibilities of Corporate Board of Directors." Free Management Library. Accessed August 1, 2021. https://managementhelp.org/boards/responsibilities.htm.

Miller, Michelle M. "Share Price Reactions to Work-Life Family Initiatives: Institutional Perspective." Academy of Management. November 20, 2017. https://journals.aom.org/doi/10.5465/30040641.

Mlitz, Kimberly. "Global telework state and trend COVID 2020-2021." Statista. March 22, 2021. Accessed July 19, 2021. https://www.statista.com/statistics/1199110/remote-work-trends-covid-survey-september-december/.

Murray, Alan and David Meyer, "The most admired Fortune 500 CEO is ..." *Fortune*, May 15, 2020. https://fortune.com/2020/05/15/most-admired-fortune-500-jamie-dimon-ceo-daily/.

"National Longitudinal Surveys." U.S. Bureau of Labor Statistics. August 2019. https://www.bls.gov/nls/questions-and-answers.htm#anch41.

"Nature of Intrinsic Motivation and Interest." Motivation Science Lab. Accessed August 27, 2021. https://koumurayama.com/research.php.

"Non-Compete Agreements." Washington State

Department of Labor & Industries. Accessed August
17, 2021.
https://lni.wa.gov/workers-rights/workplace-policies/
Non-Compete-Agreements.

"Occupational Employment and Wages, May 2020,
11-1011 Chief Executives." U.S. Bureau of Labor
Statistics. Accessed July 22, 2021.
https://www.bls.gov/oes/current/oes111011.htm#(3).

"Occupational Outlook Handbook: Computer and
Information Technology Occupations." U.S. Bureau
of Labor Statistics. Accessed August 8, 2021.
https://www.bls.gov/ooh/computer-and-information-
technology/home.htm.

"Optimizing Your Resume for Applicant Tracking
Systems." Columbia University for Career Education. Accessed August 12, 2021.
https://www.careereducation.columbia.edu/
resources/optimizing-your-resume-applicant-
tracking-systems.

Pension Benefit Guaranty Corporation. Accessed
July 18, 2021.
https://www.pbgc.gov/.

Porter, Michael E. and Nitin Nohria. "How CEOs
Manage Time." *Harvard Business Review Magazine*.
July-August 2018.
https://hbr.org/2018/07/how-ceos-manage-
time#what-do-ceos-actually-do.

"Quick Facts: Total Employer Establishments, 2019." U.S. Census Bureau. Accessed July 22, 2021. https://www.census.gov/quickfacts/fact/table/US#.

Reese, Sam. "8 Conditions for Success as CEO." *smallbizdaily* (blog). September 13, 2019. https://www.smallbizdaily.com/8-conditions-success-ceo/.

Richter, Felix. "Women's Representation in Big Tech." Statista. July 1, 2021. https://www.statista.com/chart/4467/female-employees-at-tech-companies/.

Robinson, Bryan Ph.D. "The Real Reason You Drag Your Feet When A Deadline Looms: 8 Tips On How To Get To The Finish Line." *Forbes*. June 8, 2019. https://www.forbes.com/sites/bryanrobinson/2019/06/08/the-real-reason-you-drag-your-feet-when-a-deadline-looms-8-tips-on-how-to-get-to-the-finish-line/?sh=3b00d61874c6.

"Roles and Responsibilities." BoardSource. Accessed August 1, 2021. https://boardsource.org/.

"Salary History Bans." HR Dive. July 30, 2021. https://www.hrdive.com/news/salary-history-ban-states-list/516662/.

Savickas, Mark L. "The Theory and Practice of Career Construction." In *Career Development and Counseling: Putting Theory and Research to Work*, edited by Steven D. Brown & Robert W. Lent, 45/chapter 3. Hoboken: John Wiley & Sons, Inc., 2005.

"Percentage of U.S. population who currently use any social media from 2008 to 2021." Statista. April 14, 2021. https://www.statista.com/statistics/273476/percentage-of-us-population-with-a-social-network-profile/.

"Six Seconds." The Emotional Intelligence Network. Accessed August 29, 2021. https://www.6seconds.org/tools/.

Smith, Kerri. "Brain makes decisions before you even know it." *Nature* (April 2008). https://www.nature.com/articles/news.2008.751.

"SOI Bulletin Historical Table 16." Internal Revenue Service. Accessed August 1, 2021. https://www.irs.gov/statistics/soi-tax-stats-historical-table-16.

"Survey Report: Actions to Restore Stability Survey." Willis Towers Watson. August 3, 2020. https://www.willistowerswatson.com/en-US/Insights/2020/07/actions-to-restore-stability-survey.

Swant, Marty. "2020 The World's Most Valuable Brands." *Forbes*. Accessed August 29, 2021. https://www.forbes.com/the-worlds-most-valuable-brands/#4429bcf8119c.

"To Ace Your Job Interview, Get Into Character and Rehearse." *Harvard Business Review*. April 21, 2017. https://hbr.org/2017/04/to-ace-your-job-interview-get-into-character-and-rehearse.

"Top Applicant Tracking Systems Used By Enterprise & Mid-Market." ONGIG. Accessed August 12, 2021. https://blog.ongig.com/applicant-tracking-system/top-applicant-tracking-systems-ats-software-2020/.

"Top Companies Offering Sabbatical." Built In. Accessed August 21, 2021. https://builtin.com/companies/perks/sabbatical.

"Top Division Information Technology Executive Salary in Washington." salary.com. July 21, 2021. https://www.salary.com/research/salary/benchmark/top-division-information-technology-executive-salary/wa.

"Top Companies Offering Sabbatical." Built In. Accessed August 21, 2021. https://builtin.com/companies/perks/sabbatical.

Troyer, Madison. "5 Food, Beverage, and Beauty Companies That Offer Paid Sabbaticals." *ForceBrands* (blog). July 17, 2019. https://forcebrands.com/blog/companies-paid-sabbaticals/.

"University of Washington (Seattle) – Foster School of Business." FINDMBA. Accessed July 30, 2021.

https://find-mba.com/schools/usa/washington/
washington-foster.

Villalpando, Nicole. "I have worth: Dress for Success
brings confidence to women's pandemic job searches." *Austin American-Statesman*. April 18, 2021.
https://www.statesman.com/story/lifestyle/family/
2021/04/18/dress-success-austin-creates-mentorship-
program-fit-pandemic/7065160002/.

Watson, Amy. "U.S. book industry – statistics &
facts." Statista. November 10, 2020.
https://www.statista.com/topics/1177/book-
market/#dossierSummary.

"What is the role of a mentor?" Disabilities, Opportunities, Internetworking, and Technology, University of Washington. Last modified April 9, 2021.
https://www.washington.edu/doit/what-role-mentor.

Wiles, Jackie. "Top 10 Emerging Skills for the C-
Suite." Gartner. May 24, 2019.
https://www.gartner.com/smarterwithgartner/top-10-
emerging-skills-for-the-c-suite/.

Woolworth, Rick. "Great Mentors Focus on the
Whole Person, Not Just Their Career." *Harvard
Business Review*. August 9, 2019.
https://hbr.org/2019/08/great-mentors-focus-on-the-
whole-person-not-just-their-career.

# NOTES

## 1. CAREER VISION

1. Mark L. Savickas, "The Theory and Practice of Career Construction," in *Career Development and Counseling: Putting Theory and Research to Work*, ed. Steven D. Brown & Robert W. Lent (Hoboken, NJ: John Wiley & Sons, Inc., 2005), chapter 3, 45.

## 2. INDECISION: CHOOSE A PATH

1. Kerri Smith, "Brain makes decisions before you even know it," *Nature* (April 2008), https://www.nature.com/articles/news.2008.751.
2. Roy F. Baumeister and John Tierney, *Willpower: Rediscovering the Greatest Human Strength* (New York: Penguin Press, 2011).
3. Tess Brigham, "I've been a 'millennial therapist' for more than 5 years—and this is their No. 1 complaint," CNBC make it, updated July 3, 2019, https://www.cnbc.com/2019/07/02/a-millennial-therapist-brings-up-the-biggest-complaint-they-bring-up-in-therapy.html.
4. Jory MacKay, "Productivity in 2017: What we learned from analyzing 225 million hours of work time," *RescueTime* (blog), January 4, 2018, https://rescuetime.wpengine.com/225-million-hours-productivity/.
5. 16 Personalities, accessed July 17, 2021, https://www.16personalities.com/free-personality-test.

## 3. CORPORATE VERSUS STARTUP

1. Karen Bennett, "13 Surprising Companies Who Still Give Out Pensions," Cheatsheet.com, May 5, 2018, accessed July 18, 2021, https://www.cheatsheet.com/money-career/surprising-companies-give-out-pensions.html/.
2. Pension Benefit Guaranty Corporation, accessed July 18, 2021, https://www.pbgc.gov/.

3. "Startup Failure Rate: Ultimate Report + Infographic [2021]," Nicolas Cerdeira and Kyril Kotashev, Failory, accessed July 17, 2021, https://www.failory.com/blog/startup-failure-rate.

## 4. EXECUTIVE REMOTE POSITIONS

1. Kimberly Mlitz, "Global telework state and trend COVID 2020-2021," Statista, March 22, 2021, https://www.statista.com/statistics/1199110/remote-work-trends-covid-survey-september-december/.

2. "Survey Report: Actions to Restore Stability Survey," Willis Towers Watson, August 3, 2020, https://www.willistowerswatson.com/en-US/Insights/2020/07/actions-to-restore-stability-survey.

## CAREER ROADMAP POINT #2: C-SUITE ADVICE

1. "Occupational Employment and Wages, May 2020, 11-1011 Chief Executives," U.S. Bureau of Labor Statistics, accessed July 22, 2021, https://www.bls.gov/oes/current/oes111011.htm#(3).

2. "Quick Facts: Total Employer Establishments, 2019," U.S. Census Bureau, 2019, accessed July 22, 2021, https://www.census.gov/quickfacts/fact/table/US#.

## 5. THINK LIKE A CEO

1. Alan Murray and David Meyer, "The most admired Fortune 500 CEO is ...," *Fortune*, May 15, 2020, https://fortune.com/2020/05/15/most-admired-fortune-500-jamie-dimon-ceo-daily/.

2. Elena Lytkina Botelho, Kim Rosenkoetter Powell, Stephan Kincaid, and Dina Wang, "What Sets Successful CEOs Apart," *Harvard Business Review*, May-June 2017, https://hbr.org/2017/05/what-sets-successful-ceos-apart.

3. Sam Reese, "8 Conditions for Success as CEO," *smallbizdaily* (blog), September 13, 2019, https://www.smallbizdaily.com/8-conditions-success-ceo/.

4. Jackie Wiles, "Top 10 Emerging Skills for the C-Suite," Gartner, May 24, 2019, https://www.gartner.com/smarterwithgartner/top-10-emerging-skills-for-the-c-suite/.

## 6. MENTORS & COACHES

1. "What is the role of a mentor?" Disabilities, Opportunities, Internetworking, and Technology, University of Washington, last modified April 9, 2021, https://www.washington.edu/doit/what-role-mentor.

2. Alex Bracetti, "Gallery: Tech CEOs With Their Mentors," Complex.com, Complex, July 23, 2012, accessed July 25, 2021, https://www.complex.com/pop-culture/2012/07/gallery-tech-ceos-with-their-mentors/.

3. Rick Woolworth, "Great Mentors Focus on the Whole Person, Not Just Their Career," *Harvard Business Review*, August 9, 2019, https://hbr.org/2019/08/great-mentors-focus-on-the-whole-person-not-just-their-career.

4. "Handwriting vs. Typing: How to Choose the Best Method to Take Notes," Effectiviology.com, accessed July 25, 2021, https://effectiviology.com/handwriting-vs-typing-how-to-take-notes/#Note-taking_and_your_memory.

5. "2020 ICF Global Coaching Study Executive Summary," International Coaching Federation, September 2020, https://coachingfederation.org/app/uploads/2020/09/FINAL_ICF_GCS2020_ExecutiveSummary.pdf.

6. Diane Coutu and Carol Kauffman, "What Can Coaches Do For You?" *Harvard Business Review*, last modified January 2009, https://hbr.org/2009/01/what-can-coaches-do-for-you.

## 7. INVESTING IN YOURSELF

1. Amy Watson, "U.S. book industry – statistics & facts," Statista, November 10, 2020, https://www.statista.com/topics/1177/book-market/#dossierSummary.

2. *"Encyclopædia Britannica,"* Wikipedia, accessed August 29, 2021, https://en.wikipedia.org/wiki/Encyclopædia_Britannica.

3. John B. Horrigan, "Lifelong Learning and Technology," Pew Research Center, March 22, 2016, https://www.pewresearch.org/internet/2016/03/22/lifelong-learning-and-technology/.

4. Ilana Kowarski, "What an Executive MBA Is and Reasons to Get One," *U.S. News & World Report*, November 14, 2019, https://www.usnews.com/education/best-graduate-schools/top-business-schools/articles/what-an-executive-mba-is-and-how-it-compares-to-a-full-time-mba

5. "Best Executive MBA Programs 2021," College Consensus, September 9, 2020, https://www.collegeconsensus.com/rankings/best-emba-programs/

6. "University of Washington (Seattle) – Foster School of Business," FINDMBA, accessed July 30, 2021, https://find-mba.com/schools/usa/washington/washington-foster.

## 8. BOARDS OF DIRECTORS & PROFESSIONAL ASSOCIATIONS

1. Carter McNamara, "Overview of Roles & Responsibilities of Corporate Board of Directors," Free Management Library, accessed August 1, 2021, https://managementhelp.org/boards/responsibilities.htm.

2. "50/50 Women on Boards Gender Diversity Directory™," 50/50 Women on Boards, accessed August 1, 2021, https://5050wob.com/directory/.

3. "Roles and Responsibilities," BoardSource, accessed August 1, 2021, https://boardsource.org/.

4. Robert A. Adelson, Esq., "Executive Service on Corporate Board of Directors – Benefits, Liabilities and Compensation," *CEOWorld Magazine*, February 21, 2019, https://ceoworld.biz/2019/02/21/executive-service-on-corporate-boards-of-directors-benefits-liabilities-and-compensation/.

5. Diane Lerner, "Board of Directors Compensation: Past, Present, and Future," Harvard Law School Forum on Corporate Governance, March 14, 2017, https://corpgov.law.harvard.edu/2017/03/14/board-of-directors-compensation-past-present-and-future/.

6. "SOI Bulletin Historical Table 16," Internal Revenue Service, accessed August 1, 2021, https://www.irs.gov/statistics/soi-tax-stats-historical-table-16.

7. "2018 Membership Marketing Benchmarking Report," Marketing General Incorporated, 2018, https://nacmnet.org/wp-content/uploads/The-2018-Membership-Marketing-Benchmarking-Report-Highlighted.pdf.

8. "About IEEE," IEEE, accessed August 1, 2021, https://www.ieee.org/about/index.html.

## 9. WHAT ARE YOUR SUPERPOWERS?

1. Marty Swant, "2020 The World's Most Valuable Brands," Forbes, accessed August 29, 2021, https://www.forbes.com/the-worlds-most-valuable-brands/#4429bcf8119c.
2. "Best Global Brands 2020," Interbrand, accessed August 29, 2021, https://www.interbrand.com/best-brands/.
3. "Six Seconds," The Emotional Intelligence Network, accessed August 29, 2021, https://www.6seconds.org/tools/.
4. "10 Tips For Developing A Strong Personal Brand," Forbes, July 21, 2018, https://www.forbes.com/sites/forbesagencycouncil/2018/07/21/10-tips-for-developing-a-strong-personal-brand/?sh=13dd84a9b705.

## 10. ELEVATOR PITCH

1. "Elevator Pitch," Wikipedia, accessed August 3, 2021, https://en.wikipedia.org/wiki/Elevator_pitch.

## 11. SOCIAL MEDIA PRESENCE

1. "Percentage of U.S. population who currently use any social media from 2008 to 2021," Statista, April 14, 2021,https://www.statista.com/statistics/273476/percentage-of-us-population-with-a-social-network-profile/.
2. "71% of Hiring Decision-Makers Agree Social Media is Effective for Screening Applicants," Express Employment Professionals," October 13, 2020, https://www.expresspros.com/Newsroom/America-Employed/71-of-Hiring-Decision-Makers-Agree-Social-Media-is-Effective-for-Screening-Applicants.aspx.
3. "Global social networks ranked by numbers of user 2021," Statista, August 2, 2021, https://www.statista.com/statistics/272014/global-social-networks-ranked-by-number-of-users/.

## 12. DIVERSITY & INCLUSION

1. "Annual Estimates of the Resident Population for Selected Age Groups by Sex for the United States: April 1, 2010, to July 1, 2019," United States Census Bureau, June 25, 2020, https://www2.census.gov/programs-surveys/popest/tables/2010-2019/national/asrh/nc-est2019-agesex.xlsx.

2. Victoria A. Lipnic, "The State of Age Discrimination and Older Workers in the U.S. 50 Years After the Age Discrimination in Employment Act (ADEA)," U.S. Equal Employment Opportunity Commission, June 2018, https://www.eeoc.gov/reports/state-age-discrimination-and-older-workers-us-50-years-after-age-discrimination-employment.

3. Felix Richter, "Women's Representation in Big Tech," Statista, July 1, 2021, https://www.statista.com/chart/4467/female-employees-at-tech-companies/.

4. "Lesbian, Gay, Bisexual, and Transgender Workplace Issues (Quick Take)," Catalyst Research, June 1, 2021, https://www.catalyst.org/research/lesbian-gay-bisexual-and-transgender-workplace-issues/.

## CAREER ROADMAP POINT #4: JOB SEARCH TOOLS

1. "Occupational Outlook Handbook: Computer and Information Technology Occupations," U.S. Bureau of Labor Statistics, accessed August 8, 2021, https://www.bls.gov/ooh/computer-and-information-technology/home.htm.

## 13. EXECUTIVE RESUME

1. Ladders Contributor, "Do cover letters still matter? Here's what data shows," The Ladders, June 19, 2019, https://www.theladders.com/career-advice/do-cover-letters-still-matter-heres-what-data-shows.

## 14. LINKEDIN PROFILE

1. "About Us," LinkedIn.com, accessed August 31, 2021, https://news.linkedin.com/about-us#Statistics.

2. "Optimizing Your Resume for Applicant Tracking Systems," Columbia University for Career Education, accessed August 12, 2021, https://www.careereducation.columbia.edu/resources/optimizing-your-resume-applicant-tracking-systems.

3. "Top Applicant Tracking Systems Used By Enterprise & Mid-Market," ONGIG, accessed August 12, 2021, https://blog.ongig.com/applicant-tracking-system/top-applicant-tracking-systems-ats-software-2020/.

4. Sean Callahan, "Picture Perfect: Make A Great First Impression with Your LinkedIn Profile Photo," *LinkedIn Sales Blog* (blog), December 28, 2018, https://www.linkedin.com/business/sales/blog/b2b-sales/picture-perfect--make-a-great-first-impression-with-your-linkedi.

## 15. MASTER THE INTERVIEW

1. Gartner HR Survey Shows 86% of Organizations Are "Conducting Virtual Interviews to Hire Candidates During Corona Virus Pandemic," Gartner, April 30, 2020, https://www.gartner.com/en/newsroom/press-releases/2020-04-30-gartner-hr-survey-shows-86--of-organizations-are-cond.

2. Ben Laker, Will Godley, Selin Krudet, and Rita Trehan, "4 Tips to Nail a Virtual Job Interview," *Harvard Business Review*, March 9, 2021, https://hbr.org/2021/03/4-tips-to-nail-a-virtual-job-interview.

3. "To Ace Your Job Interview, Get Into Character and Rehearse," *Harvard Business Review*, April 21, 2017, https://hbr.org/2017/04/to-ace-your-job-interview-get-into-character-and-rehearse.

## 16. EXECUTIVE COMPENSATION

1. "Equal Pay & Opportunities Act," Washington State Department of Labor & Industries, accessed August 16, 2021, https://lni.wa.gov/workers-rights/wages/equal-pay-opportunities-act/.

2. "Is It Legal for a Prospective Employer to Verify Your Current Salary?" The Law Dictionary, accessed August 17, 2021, https://thelawdictionary.org/article/is-it-illegal-for-a-prospective-employer-to-verify-your-current-salary/.

3. "Salary History Bans," HR Dive, July 30, 2021, https://www.hrdive.com/news/salary-history-ban-states-list/516662/.

4. Dan Marcec, "Equilar | New York Times 200 Highest-Paid CEOs," Equilar, June 11, 2021, https://www.equilar.com/reports/82-equilar-new-york-times-top-200-highest-paid-ceos-2021.

5. "Top Division Information Technology Executive Salary in Washington," salary.com, July 21, 2021, https://www.salary.com/research/salary/benchmark/top-division-information-technology-executive-salary/wa.

6. Kate Dixon, *Pay UP!: Unlocking Insider Secrets of Salary Negotiation* (Portland, OR: Oceanside Press, 2020), 82.

7. "Non-Compete Agreements," Washington State Department of Labor & Industries, accessed August 17, 2021, https://lni.wa.gov/workers-rights/workplace-policies/Non-Compete-Agreements.

## 17. PROJECT PLAN

1. "National Longitudinal Surveys," U.S. Bureau of Labor Statistics, August 2019, https://www.bls.gov/nls/questions-and-answers.htm#anch41

2. "Make a Career Plan," MIT Career Advising & Professional Development, accessed August 18, 2011, https://capd.mit.edu/resources/make-a-career-plan/.

3. Nicole Villalpando, "I have worth: Dress for Success brings confidence to women's pandemic job searches," *Austin American Statesman*, April 18, 2021, https://www.statesman.com/story/lifestyle/family/2021/04/18/dress-success-austin-creates-mentorship-program-fit-pandemic/7065160002/.

4. George T. Doran, "There's a S.M.A.R.T way to write management's goals and objectives." *Management Review* 70.11 (Nov. 1981): 35.

## 18. POTENTIAL SABBATICAL

1. Soulaima Gourani, "Why Employers Should Embrace Sabbatical Leave Programs," *Forbes*, January 24, 2020, https://www.forbes.com/sites/soulaimagourani/2020/01/24/why-employers-should-embrace-sabbatical-leave-programs/?sh=7e12b8847c05.

2. Michael E. Porter and Nitin Nohria, "How CEOs Manage Time," *Harvard Business Review Magazine*, July-August 2018, https://hbr.org/2018/07/how-ceos-manage-time#what-do-ceos-actually-do.

3. Michelle M. Miller, "Share Price Reactions to Work-Life Family Initiatives: Institutional Perspective," Academy of Management, November 20, 2017, https://journals.aom.org/doi/10.5465/30040641.

4. Glassdoor Team, "14 Companies Offering Sabbaticals & Hiring Now," *Glassdoor* (blog), November 9, 2018, https://www.glassdoor.com/blog/42136-2/; Madison Troyer, "5 Food, Beverage and Beauty Companies That Offer Paid Sabbati-

cals," *ForceBrands* (blog), July 17, 2019, https://forcebrands. com/blog/companies-paid-sabbaticals/; "Top Companies Offering Sabbatical," Built In, accessed August 21, 2021, https://builtin.com/companies/perks/sabbatical.

## 19. JOB SEARCH EXECUTION

1. Wendy Kaufman, "A Successful Job Search: It's All About Networking," NPR, February 3, 2011, https://www.npr.org/ 2011/02/08/133474431/a-successful-job-search-its-all-about-networking.
2. Lou Adler, "New Survey Reveals 85% of All Jobs are Filled Via Networking," LinkedIn, February 28, 2016, https://www. linkedin.com/pulse/new-survey-reveals-85-all-jobs-filled-via-networking-lou-adler/.

## 20. MAKING YOURSELF A PRIORITY

1. Bryan Robinson, Ph.D., "The Real Reason You Drag Your Feet When A Deadline Looms: 8 Tips On How To Get To The Finish Line," *Forbes*, June 8, 2019, https://www.forbes. com/sites/bryanrobinson/2019/06/08/the-real-reason-you-drag-your-feet-when-a-deadline-looms-8-tips-on-how-to-get-to-the-finish-line/?sh=3b00d61874c6.
2. Ruth Kanfer, Connie Wanberg, and Tracy Kantrowitz, "Job search and employment: A personality-motivational analysis and meta-analytic review," *Journal of Applied Psychology* 86 (2001): 837-855.
3. "Nature of Intrinsic Motivation and Interest," Motivation Science Lab, accessed August 27, 2021, https:// koumurayama.com/research.php.
4. A.H. Maslow, "A Theory of Human Motivation," *Psychological Review*, 1943, 50, 370-396, http://www.researchhistory. org/2012/06/16/maslows-hierarchy-of-needs/.
5. "Four Motivations," Changing Minds, accessed August 28, 2021, http://changingminds.org/explanations/ motivation/four_motivations.htm.

# ACKNOWLEDGMENTS

This writing journey all started with my mother supporting my desire to be a journalist by purchasing a red hardback *Webster's Dictionary* paired with a *Roget's Thesaurus* when I was 11 years old.

It is bittersweet that Mom passed away five years ago because as an avid reader—who learned English as a second language in her 20s but did not complete high school due to the WWII invasion of the Netherlands—she would have been proud of me for ticking off the box for my writing aspirations. The irony is she would not have purchased my book online since she was wary of computers, wireless phones, and the Internet—all the things that allowed me to retire early. Mom amused me and I miss her dearly.

I want to thank my clients, colleagues, and friends for their contributions, encouragements, and endorsements: Boyd Davis, Caitlin Angeloff, Charles Chen, Cindy Childress, Don Varga, Julia Funderburk, Kate Dixon, Linda Scott, Lynn Comp, Mark Baggesen, Matt Cannell, Michael Blume, Miha Kralj, Mike O'Malley, Nigel Dessau, Padma Chukka, Scott Schwisow, Suresh Chanumolu, Sree Ratnasinghe, Steve Blume, and Teilo Berquier.

Last but not least is my husband Pat. He is an incredible mentor who has put up with my shenanigans for the past five years when I had an epiphany to come out of early retirement. To be clear, I was bored since you can't paddle board every day and drink rosé. The bonus is our marriage provides alliteration for my published author name. Monique Montanino sounds better than Monique Vrinds, correct?

# ABOUT THE AUTHOR

 **Monique Montanino** began her tech sales and marketing career in Dallas, Texas before migrating like a salmon to Seattle, Washington.

The author wore her golden handcuffs for 18 years at two Fortune 500 companies—lured by cash bonuses, stock options, pensions, and the promise of retirement insurance. It allowed her to retire early, at 55 years old, as a technology sales executive.

Monique is the founder of Resumé Tech Guru whereby she collaborates with technology executives on their job search journeys. She is a certified executive coach and obtained her BBA from The University of Texas at Austin and an MBA from St. Mary's University in San Antonio.

For tech exec career advice, you can access her monthly blog posts at *www.resumetech.guru*.

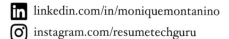 linkedin.com/in/moniquemontanino
instagram.com/resumetechguru

Printed in Great Britain
by Amazon